# The
# Austerity
# Cookbook

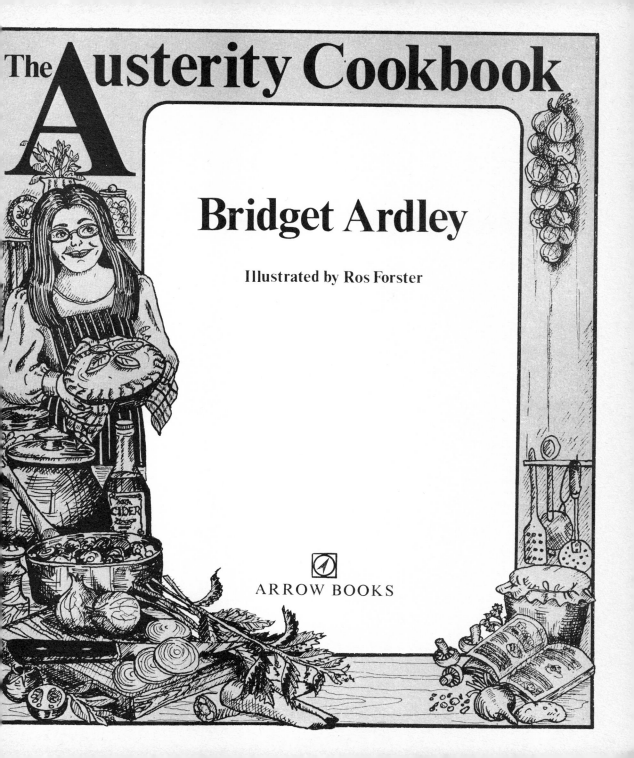

# The Austerity Cookbook

## Bridget Ardley

Illustrated by Ros Forster

ARROW BOOKS

Arrow Books Limited
3 Fitzroy Square, London W1

An imprint of the Hutchinson Publishing Group

London Melbourne Sydney Auckland
Wellington Johannesburg and agencies
throughout the world

First published Latimer New Dimensions Ltd 1975
Arrow edition July 1977
© Bridget Ardley 1975

Made and printed in Great Britain
by The Anchor Press Ltd
Tiptree, Essex

ISBN 0 09 914770 X

# Contents

To my mother

# Introduction

During the Second World War part of British official propaganda was the Ministry of Food's campaign 'On the Kitchen Front'. Housewives were constantly admonished to avoid waste, to buy and cook wisely, to eat the right food, to vary meals, and to listen to special broadcasts about buying food. There were splendid slogans like 'Let your Shopping help our Shipping', and 'Food is a munition of War — Don't Waste It!' Of course, we are not now in a state of war — fortunately; and our problems are not quite the same, for in those years food was in very short supply in Britain and strict rationing was imposed. The current problem for us is not so much one of availability but of cost — most foodstuffs are to be found in the shops but at prices which seem to increase each week. There is, however, a shortage of food in the world as a whole and it is therefore of the utmost importance that we all begin to use food as efficiently as possible — we should try to concentrate less on meat as a source of protein and try, for example, to make use of the nutritional value of plants. Much of the world's best agricultural land is given over to meat production, which is not necessarily the most productive use of it.

The war years provided something of a stimulus to the cook's ingenuity, and I suggest that now is the time to look back at the old methods of getting the very best out of food — using less but making it go further. Plan your meals for their maximum food value, as well as their taste. Try not to have left-overs, and if you do, *never* throw them away. When you prepare vegetables, throw away as little as possible — even the brown outer skins of onions can be used to give flavour to stocks and soups.

I have among my cookery books a most interesting volume called *Food and Feeding* by Sir Henry Thompson, F.R.C.S. Written in 1880, this book makes a great many points which are curiously relevant to today's problems. In his chapter on the

'Food of the English Peasant' Sir Henry says: 'At this period of our national history, when food is scarce, and the supply of meat insufficient to meet the demand which our national habits of feeding perpetuate, it is an object of the first importance to consider whether other aliments can be obtained at a cheaper rate, and at the same time equal in quality to those of the existing dietary.' He goes on to stress the importance of eggs, cheese and fish, and of pulses, or legumes, such as lentils and haricot beans, which we now know to be valuable sources of protein. Although Sir Henry has a few foibles, such as insisting that all menus should be written in French and worrying about the quality of the tobacco we smoke with our coffee, a great deal of what he says is perfectly applicable to our present situation, almost 100 years later.

For those of us who wish to continue eating meat all hope is not lost. The past few years of comparative affluence have resulted in many of the cheaper meats being unjustly denigrated. There is such prejudice against offal — or internal meats, variety meats, or whatever you like to call it. But surely we must now look to this type of meat to help to provide us with some of the protein necessary to a healthy diet. We must have protein or we may suffer from protein malnutrition — a disease found in under-developed countries. Calves' and lambs' liver tend to be expensive, but ox's and pigs' are not, and neither are hearts, kidneys, heads, tails, and feet. The last time I bought pigs' trotters they were a few pence each — and a large one is sufficient for one person. Again, during the war many ingenious ways were found of preparing offal, some of which you will find in this book. And do not let your butcher persuade you that all these kinds of meat are no longer available — animals still have the same internal organs and, while it is true that many of these find their way into pet foods, you will find that butchers who do their own butchering can

provide any part of the animal you want.

Fish has also been a victim of increased prices, for various reasons, but such valuable fish as herrings remain cheap — to quote one of my wartime cookery books: 'Everyone knows by now the fact that a good fat herring can do you as much good as a piece of beefsteak!' I'm afraid this well-known fact may now have been largely forgotten, but hopefully it will be remembered again.

Cookery books frequently lament the 'English way' with vegetables, a state of affairs which was again improved upon by the enforced austerity of the war years. Many people are now beginning to grow their own vegetables — 'Digging for Victory', perhaps. And you do not have to have a garden to be able to do this — you can grow all sorts of interesting vegetables on windowsills, balconies and patios, and there are excellent books available that will help you to do this. It is really very easy to have pots of fresh herbs in your kitchen, and is decorative as well as of enormous value in cooking.

DIG for victory NOW

I believe that a good store cupboard is essential to economic cooking — if you have to rush out at the last minute for supplies, food invariably ends up costing more. Those big glass sweet jars are excellent for storing rice, pulses and flour, and small confectioners will usually let you have them for the price of the deposit they pay to the manufacturers. Don't feel that you must banish wine from your kitchen either — there are still cheap cooking wines to be found, not perhaps of the quality one would like, but adequate. It is much less extravagant to use wine in cooking than to use the many synthetic aids to flavouring that are available. And cider is also an invaluable aid. The stock pot should again find its rightful place in the kitchen — nowadays you can freeze stock but if you don't do this, be sure to boil it up every day — and don't try to keep it going for ever. Make your own pickles and chutneys, it's easy and doesn't take long. And now that vegetable oil and olive oil are almost the same price, as are the cheapest butter and the most expensive margarine, it is up to you which you use for economic or dietary reasons.

Another major problem we face is that of keeping down fuel bills and there are ways of doing this — using a pressure cooker is one, and you should follow the instructions which come with the cooker. For the really enterprising there is the hay-box, or cosy-box, which works rather like a large thermos flask, the idea being that you bring food to boiling-point on your cooker and then transfer it to this well-insulated box where you leave it for some hours while it cooks without using any fuel at all. Hay-box cooking needs planning ahead, but it would certainly be a good way of cooking casseroles and dishes which normally take a long time. My grandmother used such a box during the First World War — hers was home-made, but I have recently seen a modern version advertised in the national press.

As for freezers as an aid to economy, I offer no advice — people that already have them give convincing arguments in favour, and people who don't have them give equally convincing arguments against. However, in view of increased fuel costs and the price of the freezers themselves, I would recommend fairly thorough research before you decide to buy.

In conclusion, I can only say that I hope you will find this collection of recipes interesting and helpful during these hard times — hard times which seem likely to be with us for quite a while. I would like to thank my friends for their encouragement and help: particularly David Barton, Sandy Carr, Ros Forster and Sue Richardson. And lastly my

husband Neil who has happily and enthusiastically acted as guinea pig and chief taster throughout.

All the recipes will give ample servings for four people unless otherwise stated.

# British and Metric Quantities

As more and more people are becoming conversant with metric units and manufacturers are using them, the quantities in this book are given in metric units as well as traditional British units. The conversions from British to metric units of weight and volume are not exact as this would otherwise result in amounts that are difficult to measure — 1 pound equals 454 grams and 1 pint equals 568 ml., for example. The metric quantities have therefore been increased by about 10 per cent, and rounded off so that 1 pint is given as 600 ml. and 1 pound as 500 grams; all other measurements are proportions of these basic equivalents. If you are using the metric quantities, you will have to increase any quantities that are given in spoons (table, dessert, or tea) proportionally — unless you have metric spoons. The metric quantities are therefore just as easy to use as British quantities but result in amounts which are about 10 per cent greater. Concerning cooking times, of course these are always approximate as cookers vary — something may take half an hour to cook in one person's cooker and forty minutes in another: this is something which cooks find out about as they get used to their own equipment. Therefore, no increase in time is given for those who are using metric quantities — this will have to be judged by the individual cook. All cooking temperatures are given in both degrees Fahrenheit and Centigrade (or Celsius), as well as in gas marks.

| WEIGHT | | | VOLUME | | | LENGTH | | |
|---|---|---|---|---|---|---|---|---|
| 2 lb. | = | 1,000 g. (1 kg.) | 1 quart | = | 1,200 ml. | 1 foot | = | 30 cm. |
| 1 lb. | = | 500 g. | | | (1.2 litres) | 6 inches | = | 15 cm. |
| 12 oz. | = | 360 g. | 1 pint | = | 600 ml. | 2 inches | = | 5 cm. |
| 10 oz. | = | 300 g. | ½ pint | = | 300 ml. | 1 inch | = | 2.5 cm. |
| 8 oz. | = | 250 g. | ¼ pint (1 gill) | = | 150 ml. | ½ inch | = | 1 cm. |
| 6 oz. | = | 180 g. | 1 tablespoon | = | 15 ml. | | | |
| 4 oz. | = | 120 g. | 1 dessertspoon | = | 10 ml. | | | |
| 2 oz. | = | 60 g. | 1 teaspoon | = | 5 ml. | | | |
| 1 oz. | = | 30 g. | | | | | | |
| ½ oz. | = | 15 g. | | | | | | |

# Oven Temperatures

## TEMPERATURE

| Gas | Fahrenheit | Centigrade (Celsius) |
|---|---|---|
| ¼ | 225°F. | 110°C. |
| ½ | 250°F. | 130°C. |
| 1 | 275°F. | 140°C. |
| 2 | 300°F. | 150°C. |
| 3 | 325°F. | 170°C. |
| 4 | 350°F. | 180°C. |
| 5 | 375°F. | 190°C. |
| 6 | 400°F. | 200°C. |
| 7 | 425°F. | 220°C. |
| 8 | 450°F. | 230°C. |
| 9 | 475°F. | 240°C. |

# Hors d'Oeuvres

## & Soups

It could be argued that, in times of real austerity, the hors d'oeuvre, and even the soup, should be dispensed with. However, this part of the meal has an important function: not only does it whet the appetite for what is to follow and reassure guests as to the quality of the rest of the meal, but it is also a splendid vehicle for making use of left-overs, for serving vegetables in their most nutritious state — raw — and for making a little go a long way. It is possible to make terrines and potted meats from the cheapest cuts of meat and from offal, and to store them, thus avoiding expensive last-minute shopping for unexpected guests. Obviously, in the interests of economy, vegetables should be used only in season, and recipes chosen to make use of the cheapest meat or fish available at the time. And bear in mind that, if you serve a filling and nutritious soup as your first course, you can get away with a smaller main course. Also, if you cook with gas you can avoid using too much fuel in the cooking of soups which may require a long time: when soup has been brought to the boil it may be simmered in a casserole in the bottom of the oven while other dishes are being cooked in the upper part of the oven. This does not apply to electric ovens where the heat is very even, unless they are already set at a low temperature.

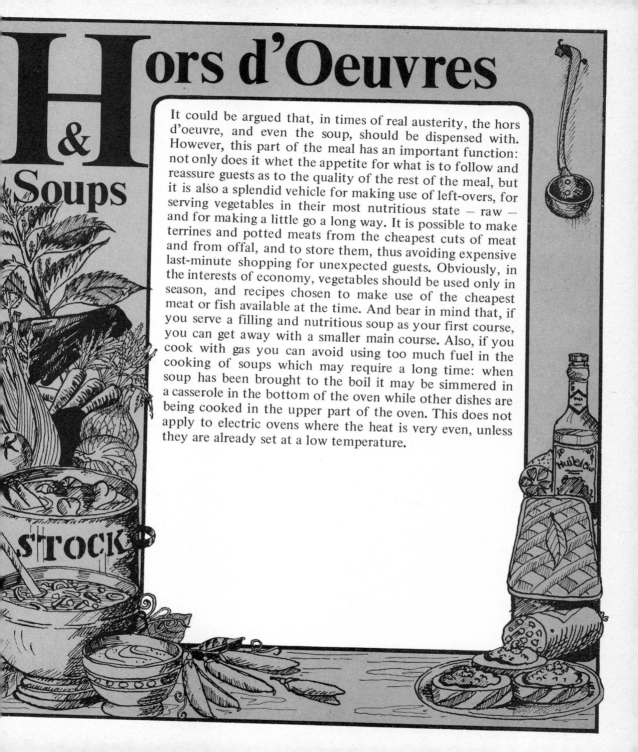

STOCK

# Savoury Fish

*This makes a good hors d'oeuvre or a lunch-time snack. A small quantity of fish is required and very little white sauce.*

Left-over white fish (about 4 oz. or 120 g.)
2 tablespoons white sauce
1 dessertspoon capers (chopped)
½ teaspoon chopped parsley
½ teaspoon vinegar
Pinch of cayenne
Salt and pepper
4 pieces buttered toast
Browned breadcrumbs (see page 171)

Flake the fish and mix it with the sauce. Stir in the capers, parsley, vinegar, cayenne, salt and pepper. Pile the mixture on to the toast, sprinkle with browned breadcrumbs, heat under the grill and serve at once.

# Anchovies and Brown Lentils

*A little extravagant if you use eggs, but these can be reduced in number, or even omitted. Brown lentils can be obtained in most health food shops. This could also be served as main course.*

½ lb. (250 g.) brown lentils
1 onion
1 tin flat anchovy fillets
2 cloves garlic
2 oz. (60 g.) butter
Salt and pepper
4 hard-boiled eggs (optional)

Soak the lentils for 2 hours and remove any bits which float to the top. Chop the onion roughly, mix it with the strained lentils and simmer in fresh water for about 1 hour, being careful not to let the lentils get mushy. Drain. Pour the oil off the anchovies and mash them to a pulp. Melt 1 oz. (30 g.) butter in a fireproof dish and stir in the lentils and onion with the crushed garlic. When this mixture is thoroughly heated, stir in the anchovies and the rest of the butter, making sure they are thoroughly mixed. Season with salt and pepper, and garnish with sliced hard-boiled eggs.

# Anchoïade

*This is always a favourite, and can be made as a quick lunch dish, as well as for an hors d'oeuvre. It is not expensive, as the quantities given below will provide a first course for four, or a lunch snack for two.*

1 long French loaf
1 tin flat fillets of anchovies in
    olive oil
2 cloves garlic
A few drops lemon juice
Freshly milled black pepper
1 egg (optional)
1 dessertspoon tomato purée
    (optional)

Crush or mince the garlic finely. Mash the anchovies to a paste, adding a little extra olive oil if you think it is necessary. Mix in the lemon juice and pepper, and add the beaten egg and the tomato purée. The mixture should be of a spreading consistency. Slice the bread thickly (I usually allow two or three slices per person, depending on what is to follow). Toast the bread on one side only and spread the paste on the untoasted side, pressing it well in. Heat under a very hot grill for about 5 minutes. Serve at once on a dish garnished with plenty of parsley.

# Kipper Pâté

*A really delicious start to a meal, but a bit extravagant on butter, so if times are really hard, halve the quantity. Do use unsalted butter or the finished dish will be far too salty.*

½ lb. (250 g.) kipper fillets
Juice of half a lemon
2 tablespoons tomato purée
4 oz. (120 g.) unsalted butter
Pepper

Skin the kippers and pound them to a paste. Soften the butter, but do not melt it, and add it with the lemon juice, tomato purée and pepper to the kippers. Stir and pound until the mixture is very smooth and pile it into a dish. Serve very cold and garnished with a few capers, olives or whatever you like.

*Note:* A similar and delicious variation on the above can be made using a tin of tuna instead of the kippers, and omitting the tomato purée.

15

# Liver Pâté

*Of the many, many recipes for liver pâté, this is the one that I have found to be the most economical and successful. It is always a favourite, and impresses people no end when served as an hors d'oeuvre. We also take it on picnics, serve it at parties, and eat it with other cold meats and salad for lunch. If you have some white wine you can moisten the mixture with a small glass, but this is by no means essential.*

1 lb. (500 g.) of the cheapest liver
¾ lb. (360 g.) fat green bacon pieces
1 tablespoon chopped fried onion
    (optional)
1 clove garlic, minced (optional —
    but desirable)
¼ level teaspoon ground black
    pepper
½ level teaspoon ground mace
Pinch ground nutmeg
1 small glass white wine (optional)
About ½ lb. (250 g.) thinly sliced
    streaky bacon (try to get straight
    rashers — they are easier to
    manage)

Wash the liver and remove the skin and any coarse tubes. Remove rinds from all the bacon. Mince the liver and the fat bacon together — if you like your pâté to have a coarse texture, you need only mince it once, if not, pass it through the mincer two or three times. If you are using onion and garlic, mix it well into the meat mixture. Add the pepper, mace and nutmeg, and make sure they are thoroughly distributed throughout the mixture. Add the wine and mix well. Line a 1 lb. (500 g.) loaf tin with the streaky bacon, and pack in the liver mixture. Then fold the bacon over the top so that the meat is completely enclosed. Cover with foil and stand the tin in a baking tin containing about 1 in. of water and bake in a moderate oven (Gas mark 4, Electric 350ºF., 180ºC.) for about one hour. You can tell when it is ready because it starts to shrink away from the sides of the tin. Leave it to cool in the tin, with a weight on top, and turn it out when it is completely cold. Slice thinly, or allow people to serve themselves.

# Poor Man's Liver Pâté

½ lb. (250 g.) liver sausage
¼ cup mayonnaise (see page 174)
1 small minced onion
¼ cup chopped walnuts (optional)
½ teaspoon oregano
Salt and freshly ground black
    pepper

*If you want something even cheaper than the preceding recipe, which takes little time to prepare, and no cooking, try this American recipe.*

Mix everything into a paste and chill it before serving with toast.

# Spinach and Pork Pâté

1 lb. (500 g.) belly pork
1 lb. (500 g.) spinach
¼ teaspoon mixed spices
    (mace, allspice and cloves,
     ground in equal quantities)
Salt and freshly milled
    black pepper

*A light pâté which can be served hot as a main dish, but it is better cold as an hors d'oeuvre, with toast. And it is worth remembering that spinach is very nutritious, having a high content of calcium, protein, iron and vitamins. You can use frozen, or even tinned, spinach, but fresh is best.*

Wash the spinach thoroughly in the usual way, picking out any very coarse stems and really yellow leaves. Cook it without adding any more water other than that which it has retained in the washing process. Drain it, and when it has cooled, squeeze it with your hands to remove as much moisture as possible; then chop it. Mince the meat and season it with about two teaspoons of salt, plenty of pepper and the mixed spices. Mix the meat and spinach together thoroughly and pack the mixture into a 1 lb. (500 g.) greased loaf tin. Cover it with a piece of buttered paper and stand it in a baking tin half full of water. Cook it in a very moderate oven (Gas mark 3, Electric 325°F., 170°C.) for about 1 hour. Be careful to avoid overcooking as this will make the pâté too dry.

# Spiced Breast of Lamb

*This is very cheap and easy to prepare. It can be served as an hors d'oeuvre, as a main dish with other cold meats and salads, or whenever you choose.*

To make brine boil the salt, sugar and saltpetre in the water until dissolved and put into a deep casserole to cool. Remove the bones and surplus fat from the lamb and lay them on a board skin-side down. Chop the onion and mix it with the pepper and spread this mixture over the lamb. With the two breasts, broad ends together, and starting at the narrow end of one of them, roll them up as tightly as possible. If the roll looks a bit unstable, tie it tightly with string. Sew up the ends securely with a darning needle and coarse thread so that none of the onion can escape. Put it in the brine with a plate on top to keep it under, and leave it for 2 days (check from time to time to make sure that it is completely covered). Remove it from the brine, drain it, place in clean water and simmer for 3 hours. When tender, remove it from the water and leave to cool with a weight on top (I often put it into a loaf tin, lined with foil, to cool — this gives it a good shape). When serving it, slice it very thinly.

2 breasts of lamb

1 onion

1 level teaspoon pepper

2 pints (1.2 litres) water

6 oz. (180 g.) cooking salt

2 teaspoons brown sugar

Pinch saltpetre

# Meat Sanders

*I have no idea why this is called Meat Sanders, but it is a very good way of using up left-over mashed potato and cold meat.*

Mix enough flour with the potatoes to make a rollable pastry — you may find a little milk will help if you are using left-over potato. The pastry

1 lb. (500 g.) left-over mashed
    potato ( or cook and mash
    some specially, being sure
    to add a little butter)
Flour
Cooked meat
Seasoning to taste

should be of the correct consistency to prevent cracking. Roll it to about ¼ in. thick and cut into 4 in. squares. Chop or mince the meat and season it to taste with salt and pepper, and herbs, if you wish. Put a little of the meat on to each square and seal them like sausage rolls. Brush with beaten egg and bake in the top of a moderate oven until the pastry browns.

## Potted Meat

½ lb. (250 g.) cooked meat
2 oz. (60 g.) cooked fat bacon
    (or ham)
Salt and pepper
1 teaspoonful mixed spice
1 teaspoon made mustard
1 or 2 oz. (30–60 g.) butter

*Very tasty – an excellent start to a meal and one which can be made entirely from left-overs.*

Remove all skin, gristle and sinew from the meat, and mince it with the bacon. For a finer texture, put it through the mincer twice. Put it into a basin and add the spice, salt and pepper, and the mustard. Melt the butter and add about two thirds of it to the meat. Mix all together very thoroughly, pack into individual pots or a straight-sided casserole, and seal with the remaining butter.

## Potted Chicken

10 oz. (300 g.) cooked chicken
1 oz. (30 g.) cooked bacon
2 oz. (60 g.) butter
1 teaspoon lemon juice
Salt
Paprika
1 pinch mixed herbs (dried)

*This only takes about five minutes to cook, and if properly sealed, will keep for up to ten days in a fridge. It is a good way of using up cooked chicken, and 10 oz. (300 g.) will make sufficient for four people.*

Chop the chicken and bacon finely (or mince if you prefer a finer texture). Heat three quarters of the butter and stir in the chicken, bacon, lemon juice, salt and paprika to taste, and the herbs. Cook gently for about 3 minutes and pack into a small terrine or straight-sided casserole. Heat the remaining butter until it is foaming and strain it over the meat to form a seal.

# Rillettes de Porc

*A lovely hors d'oeuvre which, though it does take some time to prepare, is very economical and keeps well. When we ate this in southern France a large jar of rillettes was placed on the table from which we were free to help ourselves — only the thought of what was to follow prevented us from being very greedy.*

Ask the butcher to remove the rind and the bones from the pork — if he is unobliging it is not very difficult to do it yourself. Rub the meat well with salt and leave it to stand for about 6 hours. Then cut it into very small pieces — a little bigger than a match is about right. Pack the meat into an earthenware casserole with the fat also cut into small pieces. Crush the garlic and bury it, together with the bouquet in the middle of the meat. Sprinkle with a little black pepper, add about ¼ pint (150 ml.) water, and cook with the lid on for about 4 hours in a very low oven (Gas mark 1, Electric 275°F., 140°C.). At this stage the meat will look rather unappetising as it swims in fat, but do not be put off. Taste to see if more pepper and salt are needed — *rillettes* should be rather well-seasoned. Turn the meat into a sieve, with a bowl underneath to catch the fat. Leave to drain for about ½ hour. When well-drained, pull the meat to pieces with two forks so that it is really finely shredded. I think it is then best to pack the meat into several small jars — if you use one big jar the seal will be broken each time you want to serve the *rillettes*. When the jars are full strain the fat over them, trying to leave any meat juices behind and filling each jar right to the top. Cover the jars with foil lids and store in a fridge or cool larder.

2 lb. (1 kg.) belly pork
1 lb. (500 g.) pork fat
1 clove garlic
*Bouquet* of fresh herbs
Black pepper

# Mushrooms with Coriander

*This is rather like Mushrooms à la grecque, but is easier to make. It is best to use olive oil, but in the interests of economy, you can use any other vegetable oil.*

Rinse the mushrooms and dry them in a clean cloth. Do not peel them, but slice them into quarters, with the stalks neatly trimmed. Squeeze the lemon juice over them. Warm the oil in a heavy pan and put in the lightly crushed coriander seeds. Heat for about 1 minute. Keeping the heat low, put in the mushrooms and the bay leaf, and the seasoning. Cook the mushrooms for about 1 minute, cover the pan, and leave to cook on a very low heat for about 5 minutes. Allow to get completely cold before serving.

8 oz. (250 g.) of small white
mushrooms
1 teaspoon coriander seeds
2 tablespoons oil
Lemon juice
Salt and pepper
One bay leaf

# Raw Vegetables

*This hors d'oeuvre (les crudités in French) can look very attractive if care is taken, and, if a good mixture of vegetables is chosen, it will be both appetising and nutritious. The following is merely a guide and variations can be made according to availability and taste. I usually assemble it on a large tray in a number of small dishes.*

Thinly sliced tomatoes and cucumber (dressed with a little oil, lemon juice, salt and black pepper), radishes, young white celery (cut into small strips), very small broad beans (sprinkled with salt), thinly sliced red or green peppers (dressed with a little oil), finely grated carrots (mixed with a vinaigrette dressing, adding sugar if the carrots are not very young).
Accompany these with mayonnaise (p. 174), salami, ham, anchovies or whatever is available.

# Iced Cucumber (1)

*Very good in hot weather, when young cucumbers are readily available.*

1 cucumber
Mint
Iced salted water

Peel the cucumber and slice lengthways. For each person, fill a small bowl with iced salted water, put in 2 ice cubes, 3 mint leaves and a few slices of cucumber.

# Iced Cucumber (2)

*More elaborate than (1), and needing more cucumbers, so make it when they are at their cheapest.*

2 cucumbers
½ onion
1 dessertspoon lemon juice
Salt and pepper
Good handful fresh mint,
   finely chopped
½ pint (300 ml.) prawns or
   shrimps (optional)
½ pint (300 ml.) aspic jelly
   (see page 169)

Grate the cucumber and onion as finely as possible and mix thoroughly with the mint and lemon juice. Season with salt and pepper to taste. Stir in the aspic jelly. Chill and serve garnished with prawns or whole mint leaves.

# Iced Cucumber (3)

*This is sometimes known as raita and is frequently used as an accompaniment to curry.*

1 cucumber
1 pint (600 ml.) natural
   yoghurt (p. 168)
1 crushed clove of garlic
1 teaspoon chopped fresh mint
Salt and pepper

Peel and slice or grate the cucumber. Add to the yoghurt mixed with the crushed garlic and mint and seasoned to taste. Thin with a little milk if preferred and chill well before serving.

# A Useful Stock

*This can be made in fairly large quantities as it will keep well in a fridge (you can even freeze it, should you wish to). It does not have a strong flavour, but will add richness to soup, stews and some sauces. There is no need to season it — rather season the dish to which it is added.*

Scraps of meat, if available
Calf's Foot or pig's trotter
    (optional — but worth
    trying to get)
Marrow bones
Water

Split the foot or trotter, or ask the butcher to do it for you. Put all the bones and meat into a large pan and cover with cold water. Bring slowly to the boil and remove the scum which will rise to the surface. When the scum has cleared reduce the heat, cover and simmer gently for about two hours. (Remember that at least part of this simmering can be done in the bottom of a gas oven while something else is cooking.) When cooked, sieve and allow to cool. When cold, the fat can be removed from the jelly.

# Strong Celery Soup

*As this tastes very strongly of the vegetable, it would be as well to make sure that any guests do like celery. It is very easy to make, and if the celery is small and young the whole head should be used, including the leaves.*

1 head celery
1 potato
1 pint (600 ml.) milk *
1 pint (600 ml.) stock*
*If you cannot spare the milk,
use 2 pints (1.2 litres) stock
(see above)
Salt and pepper
Pinch nutmeg
1 oz. (30 g.) butter

Wash and chop the celery finely, including the leaves. Peel and chop the potato. Melt the butter, and stew the vegetables very gently for about five minutes. Add the stock, but not the milk, bring to the boil and simmer for about ¾ hour, until the celery is tender. Sieve, or liquidize, add the milk and reheat gently. Add the nutmeg and salt and pepper to taste.

# Jerusalem Artichoke Soup

1 lb. (500 g.) artichokes
1½ pints (900 ml.) water
½ pint (300 ml.) stock (see
    page 23)
1 oz. (30 g.) butter
Top of the milk (or cream, if
    available)
Salt and pepper to taste
Pinch of nutmeg

*Jerusalem artichokes are somewhat fiddly to peel, but they taste so nice that they are worth the effort.*

Peel and slice the artichokes and stew them gently in the butter for five minutes. Add the water, stock, salt, pepper and nutmeg and simmer for about ¾ hour. Sieve, and reheat very gently, but do not boil. Adjust the seasoning and stir in the cream just before serving.

# Nettle Soup

1 lb. (500 g.) nettles
1 onion
3 potatoes
1 pint (600 ml.) stock
½ pint (300 ml.) milk
1 dessertspoon plain yoghurt
    (or top of the milk if no
    yoghurt available)
Salt and pepper

*If you live in the country you should have no trouble finding the main ingredient for this soup. If in a town, nettles are often to be found in waste places, or in parks (ask the park keeper's permission!). Gather the nettles when they are young — and do wear gloves.*

Remove the stalks from the nettles and wash the leaves thoroughly (still wearing gloves). Put them in a saucepan with the sliced onion and potatoes, the stock and seasoning, and simmer gently for ½ hour. Sieve and return to the pan with the milk and bring to the boil. Just before serving, add the yoghurt and adjust the seasoning to taste.

# Carrot Cream Soup

*As well as tasting good, this soup has a pleasing appearance, and, of course, a high vitamin content. It is based on a wartime recipe.*

1 lb. (500 g.) carrots
1 large onion
1 pint (600 ml.) milk
½ pint (300 ml.) well-flavoured
    vegetable stock
1 tablespoon chopped parsley

Boil the carrots until tender. Chop the onion and stew it separately in a little of the milk. Add to the carrots and sieve, or liquidize. Add the rest of the milk, and reheat while stirring. Serve with the parsley sprinkled on top.

# Carrot Soup

*This is a clear soup, using fewer carrots than the one above, and no milk.*

½ lb. (250 g.) carrots
2 sticks celery
1 pint (600 ml.) water
½ pint (300 ml.) well-flavoured
    meat stock
1 crust stale bread
Salt and pepper to taste
Pinch sugar
Oil

Slice the carrots and celery into small pieces. Stew for five minutes in 1 dessertspoon of oil. Add the water, stock, bread, salt and pepper, and sugar. Cook until the vegetables are soft and rub through a sieve or liquidize. Reheat and serve with a sprinkling of chopped parsley or mint.

# Watercress Soup (1)

1 lb. (500 g.) potatoes
1 bunch watercress
2 pints (1.2 litres) cold water
¼ pint (150 ml.) milk or cream
½ oz. (15 g.) butter
Salt and pepper

Peel and boil the potatoes in the water until they are almost cooked, then add the washed and chopped watercress (keeping a little aside). Bring to the boil again and cook until the potatoes are quite soft. Sieve and reheat, adding the milk or cream, the butter and salt and pepper to taste. Serve with a sprinkling of chopped watercress on top.

# Watercress Soup (2)

*A less economical version of this delicious soup than (1) above, but very good.*

1½ lbs. (750 g.) potatoes
2 leeks
1 bunch watercress
2 oz. (60 g.) butter
2 pints (1.2 litres) water
1 egg yolk
1 tablespoon milk
Salt and pepper

Peel the potatoes, clean the leeks and wash the watercress. Chop them all and cook together in the melted butter for about 5 minutes. Add the salt and pepper, and water, bring to the boil and simmer for 20 minutes. Taste and adjust seasoning if necessary. Beat the egg yolk in the milk, remove the soup from the heat and stir in the egg mixture before serving.

# Pea Pod Soup

*Do not serve this in the same meal as the peas, and use only good green pods from young peas, otherwise they may be stringy, and the soup an unattractive colour.*

1 or 2 carrots
Pea pods (from 1 lb. (500 g.) peas)
1 onion
1 stick celery (or the leaves from
    a young head of celery)
2 or 3 sprigs mint
1 oz. (30 g.) butter
Salt and pepper

Wash the pods, chop and cover with water. Simmer for about 1½ hours or until they are tender. Sieve or liquidize them. Chop the onion and celery, grate the carrots and cook them gently in butter for about 15 minutes. Stir in the pea pod stock, season to taste, and serve sprinkled with chopped mint.

# Basque Peasant Soup

*Very cheap, and delicious. It takes a long time to cook, because of the beans, so, once again, if you cook with gas try to make it when you have the oven on for something else, so that it can do part of its simmering in a casserole.*

1 large onion
1 small white cabbage

Soak the haricot beans overnight. Slice the onion and sauté it in the fat in a large saucepan. Add the

½ lb. (250 g.) haricot beans
2 cloves garlic
Salt and pepper
Pork fat, if available (otherwise
   cooking oil)

cabbage cut into fine strips, the beans and the crushed garlic. Add salt and pepper to taste and cover with 4 pints (2.5 litres) of water. Simmer for at least 3 hours. Very good served with warm French bread.

# Cheese Soup

*This recipe was popular during the First World War. It is rather unusual, and care should be taken that cheese is not used in any other dish in the meal.*

1 oz. (30 g.) butter
1 oz. (30 g.) flour
¼ lb. (120 g.) cheese
2 eggs
1 pint (600 ml.) milk
Salt and pepper
Chopped parsley

Separate the eggs, beat the yolks and whisk the whites until stiff. Make a white sauce with the butter, flour and milk and when cool add the egg yolks, grated cheese and seasoning. Do not use as much salt as usual, as this is to some extent provided by the cheese. Carefully stir the parsley into the egg whites. Reheat the sauce, being careful not to let it boil, and pour it carefully over the egg whites. Serve at once with brown bread.

# Finnie Soup

*Very economical, and you will find that most fish-mongers will give you fish heads and scraps for a few pence (or even for nothing).*

½ lb. (250 g.) whiting
Any fish heads and scraps
   available
1 onion
1 potato
1 pint (600 ml.) water
1 pint (600 ml.) milk
Salt and pepper
Pinch nutmeg
1 oz. (30 g.) butter

Peel and chop the onion and potato and stew them very gently in the butter for about 10 minutes. Add the fish, heads and scraps, and the water. Bring to the boil, and simmer for an hour. Lift off the bones and skin, which will have risen to the surface, and pass the remainder through a sieve. Reheat, add the milk, and salt, pepper and nutmeg to taste. Simmer for a further ten minutes, and, if you wish, sprinkle with a little grated cheese and chopped parsley before serving.

# Leek and Potato Soup

*Very easy to prepare, and makes use of the coarsest tops of leeks, and only one potato.*

Left-over green tops of leeks
1 potato
1 pint (600 ml.) vegetable stock
½ pint (300 ml.) milk
Salt and pepper
Pinch nutmeg

Wash the leek green free from grit and chop it up very finely with the peeled potato. Put it into a saucepan with the stock and milk, and add the salt, pepper and nutmeg. Simmer gently for ¾ hour, rub through a sieve, or liquidize, reheat and serve with a sprinkling of parsley or chopped chives.

# French Vegetable Soup

*This is adapted from a war-time recipe — it is very tasty, highly nutritious and sufficiently filling for a lunch dish. When using it to start a meal, you need only provide something light to follow it.*

1 clove garlic
2 onions
1 or 2 leeks
1 carrot
1 turnip
½ parsnip
½ small white cabbage
½ large cooking apple
2 or 3 mushrooms
Small head celery
1 bay leaf
Branch fresh thyme (½ teaspoon dried)
2 pints (1.2 litres) stock (see page 23)
Salt and pepper
Oil

Crush the garlic. Coarsely chop the onions and dice the carrots, parsnip and turnip. Put the oil in a large pan and add the garlic, onions, carrots, parsnip and turnip. Cook for a few minutes stirring constantly. Now add the chopped celery, leeks, cabbage and apple, the bay leaf, thyme and seasoning. Cover with stock and simmer for about ¾ hour with a lid on. Wash and chop the mushrooms (no need to peel) and cook them in a little oil. When cooked, stir them into the soup and serve.

# Italian Vegetable Soup

*This is a useful way of using up the odd vegetables that tend to accumulate in the bottom of the vegetable rack.*

Any vegetables
e.g. 1 potato
    1 onion
    1 carrot
    ½ dozen sprouts
    1 tomato
1 clove garlic
1 bone (preferably bacon)
Handful of macaroni or broken-up
    spaghetti
Chopped up left-over cold meat
    (optional)
1 sage leaf (or a pinch of dried
    sage)

Chop all the vegetables and the garlic into very small pieces and put them, with the bone, into a saucepan. Cover with 1 pint (600 ml.) of water and simmer gently for one hour. Add the macaroni and meat and simmer for another ½ hour. Remove the bone and serve sprinkled with grated cheese.

# Chicken Broth

*A way of using up the carcase and giblets of a chicken. Don't omit the spices as they give a delicious flavour.*

Carcase and giblets of 1 chicken
2 pints (1.2 litres) water
1 oz. (30 g.) rice or pearl barley
1 onion
1 stick celery
6 peppercorns
1 blade mace
Salt
1 teaspoon chopped parsley

Break up the carcase and scald and chop the giblets. Put everything except the parsley into a large saucepan with the water, bring to the boil and simmer with a lid on for 2 hours. Strain and reheat. Adjust seasoning to taste and sprinkle with parsley before serving.

# Rice Soup

*A rather bland soup, and most appropriate before a highly flavoured main dish. It is very good as it is, but a handful of diced cooked meat of almost any kind may be added for the last 10 minutes of cooking.*

2 oz. (60 g.) rice

1 onion

1½ pints (900 ml.) vegetable
　　stock

¼ pint (150 ml.) milk

1 oz. (30 g.) flour

1 oz. (30 g.) fat or oil

2 cloves

Pinch nutmeg

Salt and pepper.

Melt the fat in a saucepan and add the washed rice. Stir for 5 minutes, but do not allow the rice to brown. Add the stock and bring to the boil. Stick the cloves in the onion. Remove any scum from the rice and add the onion. Simmer gently until the rice is soft. Blend the flour with the milk and stir it into the rice. Boil for 10 minutes stirring all the time. Remove the onion, and add nutmeg, salt and pepper to taste.

*Note:* Stirring is important in this recipe to prevent the rice from sticking.

# Oatmeal Soup

*This may sound a bit like gruel but don't worry, it is very tasty. As for Rice Soup, a little diced cooked meat may be added, if desired. Rolled oats can be used instead of oatmeal.*

2 oz. (60 g.) medium oatmeal

2 pints (1.2 litres) vegetable stock

1 onion

1 carrot

1 leek

¼ pint (150 ml.) milk

Branch of fresh marjoram (or
　　½ teaspoon dried)

Salt and pepper

Grate the carrot and chop the onion and leek finely (or mince). Melt the fat and stir in the oatmeal. Stir for 5 minutes. Add the stock and the vegetables and marjoram. Stir until it boils and simmer for 45 minutes. Season to taste and stir in the milk. Re-boil and serve with a sprinkling of chopped chives or parsley.

# Split Pea Soup

*Very tasty and filling, this soup makes use of those parts of a head of celery which are often thrown away. The quantities given here will make about 4 pints (2.5 litres) of soup.*

1 lb. (500 g.) split peas

2 onions

Green tops and outside sticks of
    a head of celery

1 teaspoon salt

½ teaspoon pepper

4 pints (2.5 litres) water or stock

Bacon rinds

1 turnip

2 carrots

Wash and soak the peas for 12–24 hours. Slice the onions thinly and chop the celery, turnip and carrots. Put the peas and vegetables in the water or stock with the salt, pepper and bacon rinds. Simmer gently for about 1½ hours or until the peas are soft. Remove the bacon rinds and sieve. Reheat and serve.

# Barley Cream Soup

*A thick, tasty and nutritious soup; the sherry is, of course, optional, but a very good addition for special occasions. It does take some time to cook, but the resulting soup is so good that it is worthwhile.*

2 oz. (60 g.) pearl barley

1 small carrot

1 small onion

1 stick celery

1 oz. (30 g.) butter

2 pints (1.2 litres) stock

1 egg

¼ pint (150 ml.) milk

1 tablespoon sherry (optional)

Salt and pepper

Wash the barley and put it in a pan covered with cold water. Bring to the boil, strain, and rinse in cold water. Melt the butter and cook the chopped vegetables in it for a few minutes with the lid on, shaking occasionally. Add the barley, stock, salt and pepper, bring to the boil and simmer for 2 hours. Beat the egg and milk together and stir into the strained soup. Reheat slowly, but do not boil. Add the sherry and adjust the seasoning before serving.

# Calf's Foot Soup

*Ask your butcher to chop up the calf's foot for you.*

1 calf's foot
4 sticks celery
1 small onion
1 sprig parsley
1 sprig thyme
3 pints (1.8 litres) water
Salt and pepper
Chopped parsley (to garnish)

Wash the calf's foot pieces. Slice the celery and peel the onion. Put all the ingredients into a pan, except the seasoning and chopped parsley. Bring to the boil and simmer gently for about 3 hours. Strain, re-heat and season to taste. Serve with a sprinkling of chopped parsley. This soup may be kept hot for some time, or re-heated without spoiling.

# Lettuce Soup

*A simple soup which takes only a short time to prepare. Sorrel can be used instead of lettuce, or half lettuce and half sorrel.*

1 medium-sized lettuce
2 pints (1.2 litres) chicken or
    vegetable stock
1 tablespoon rice
1 oz. (30 g.) butter

Shred the lettuce as finely as you can. Melt the butter in a saucepan and cook the lettuce gently for 10 minutes. Add the stock and rice and cook slowly until the rice is tender.

# Eggs & Cheese

Although eggs sometimes tend to be expensive nowadays, it is worth remembering that they are a valuable food, and being rich in protein, they can be an excellent substitute for meat which is even more expensive. It is said that as they lack starch, they should be combined with farinaceous foods to give a balanced diet, but unless you intend to abandon meat altogether, this is not too serious a problem. During the last war, it was fairly common to preserve fresh eggs when they were available — I well remember buckets of eggs in water-glass in our larder at home, which were used instead of dried eggs on very special occasions. If you should want to try preserving fresh eggs, water-glass can still be obtained and directions for its use will be given by the manufacturer. As cheese is a product of milk, it too is a valuable food and is frequently recommended as a meat substitute. It is supposed to be a more concentrated form of nourishment than best beef. Apart from all this, it also tastes good, and some excellent dishes can be prepared with it. Do not throw away any dried-up pieces of cheese — these are very good for grating. If you want to dry cheese for grating, keep it in a cool, dry place exposed to the air. Hang it up in muslin or keep it on a plate and turn it now and then to prevent mould from forming. If it does get a coating of mould, it can still be used, as long as the mould is scraped off. Store grated cheese in a screw-topped jar and use as required. Neither eggs nor cheese usually require a lot of cooking, so they are also economical in the use of fuel.

# Shirred Eggs

2 eggs per person
3 oz. (90 g.) grated cheese
    (Cheddar, or any of the
    firm English cheeses)
1 oz. (30 g.) butter
Salt and pepper
½ tablespoon chopped parsley

*A very good lunch snack, making use of both eggs and cheese, and excellent served with a fresh green salad.*

Spread the butter over the bottom and sides of a shallow fireproof dish and sprinkle half the cheese evenly in the bottom. Carefully break the eggs on top and season with salt and pepper. Mix the parsley with the remainder of the cheese, and sprinkle carefully over the eggs. Cook in a moderate oven (Gas mark 4, Electric 350°F. 180°C.) for 15 to 20 minutes, until the eggs have set and are light brown.

# Eggs à la Monteynard

4 eggs
½ lb. (250 g.) rice
4 tablespoons Gruyère or
    Emmenthal cheese
½ pint (300 ml.) stock
1 oz. (30 g.) butter
Salt and pepper

*Another substantial dish, which can be preceded by a light hors d'oeuvre and followed by salad. Slightly more expensive, as it uses Gruyère or Emmenthal cheese, but the quantities given are ample for four people.*

Boil the rice in the usual way, but only for ¼ of its cooking time, then drain it, add the stock and continue to cook it until it is ready. In the meantime, soft-boil the eggs (five minutes, then put in cold water). Shell the eggs carefully. Butter a shallow fireproof dish. The rice, when ready, should have absorbed all the stock and should be put into the dish. With the back of a tablespoon, make egg-shaped dents in the rice and place a half egg into each (be very careful when you halve the eggs, as the yolks should be runny). Sprinkle with salt and pepper and spread the grated cheese over the top – put an extra layer of cheese on each half egg. Melt the butter and pour it over the dish. Put in a hot oven (Gas mark 8, Electric 450°F., 230°C.) for no more than 3 minutes, so that the cheese will have melted but the egg yolks will still be soft.

# Convent Eggs

*A recipe which is to be found with a number of names and methods. This is my favourite, both in name and method.*

2 hard-boiled eggs
½ pint (300 ml.) milk
1 oz. (30 g.) butter
1 oz. (30 g.) flour
1 onion
Salt and pepper
Browned breadcrumbs

Slice the onion into thin rounds and cook for about five minutes in the butter. Add the milk and flour gradually, and cook for 3 minutes, stirring all the time so that there are no lumps. Carefully slice the eggs as thinly as you can without breaking them. Turn the onion mixture into a fireproof dish, and arrange the egg on top. Heat sufficiently to make the egg thoroughly hot, sprinkle with browned breadcrumbs and serve.

# Pork and Potato Omelette

*This is a tasty and filling dish, which comes origin-ally from the Auvergne, where it is called Omelette Brayaude. The quantities given below will be sufficient for two or three people, and it can be served as a main course, accompanied by vegetables, or a fresh green salad.*

1 slice belly pork (about ¾ in.
   thick)
1 large potato
2 or 3 eggs
½ oz. (15 g.) butter
1 tablespoon fresh cream
1 dessertspoon finely grated
   cheese
Salt and pepper

Remove the rind from the pork and cut it into small dice. Peel and dice the potato. Using an omelette pan, heat the pork gently until the fat begins to run, then put in the potato and cook it gently until it is soft. You should shake the pan from time to time to prevent the potato from sticking — if necessary, add half the butter. In the meantime, beat the eggs thoroughly and season them with salt and pepper. When the potato and meat are cooked turn up the heat and add the rest of the butter to the pan. Put in the eggs and let them almost set as you would for an ordinary omelette. Slide onto a hot plate and pour the heated cream on top. Sprinkle with grated cheese and serve.

# Noodles

*Like so many other things, pasta has now become an expensive item — so much so that it is worth trying to make your own. Of course, it does not keep like shop-bought pasta, but it tastes better. It can be served with just melted butter and grated cheese, or with any sauce you wish. The dough can be made into lasagne by cutting it into squares instead of strips, but sprinkle fine semolina between the pieces until you cook them, or they will stick together.*

Sieve the flour onto a board, make a well in the centre, sprinkle with salt, and break in the eggs. Add the milk, and start to beat with a fork, taking in a little flour with each stroke. When most of the flour is used up, work the dough with your hands, using the remaining flour to stop it sticking to your fingers. Knead the dough thoroughly for about 15 minutes and try to avoid adding more flour or the dough will become too stiff. You should end up with a very soft dough. If it becomes dry when you are kneading it, keep moistening your fingers with milk. It is best to divide the dough into about four pieces before rolling it. Dust each piece with flour and roll it as thinly as you can. Then roll it up (like a Swiss roll) and cut it into thin slices. Unroll each slice quickly and hang the strips over the back of a chair to prevent them sticking. It is best to make the pasta the day before you want to cook it so that it can become thoroughly dry. To cook it, drop it into fast-boiling salted water to which one teaspoon oil has been added. Stir it once and allow to boil for 10 minutes. Drain it and serve according to your wishes.

2 eggs
7 oz. (200 g.) plain flour
1 teaspoon milk
Pinch salt

# Macaroni and Egg Casserole

*A very substantial meal, needing no accompaniment, simply a salad to follow.*

4½ oz. (135 g.) macaroni

3 pints (1.8 litres) boiling water

Salt

2 oz. (60 g.) oil

1¼ oz. (40 g.) flour

1 pint (600 ml.) milk

3 teaspoons dry mustard

1 teaspoon Worcestershire sauce

3 oz. (90 g.) grated cheese

8 oz. (250 g.) cooked runner beans

3 hard-boiled eggs

2 oz. (60 g.) minced onion

Cook the macaroni in the boiling salted water, drain it and rinse with clean boiling water. While it is cooking, blend the flour with the oil, stir in the milk and cook until it thickens, stirring all the time. Add the onion, mustard, pepper, sauce, and 3 teaspoons salt. Remove from the heat and stir in 2 oz. (60 g.) of the cheese. Using a fairly shallow fireproof dish, arrange layers of macaroni, beans, and sliced eggs, keeping a little egg for garnishing. Pour the sauce over and sprinkle with the rest of the cheese. Bake in a moderate oven (Gas mark 4, Electric 350°F., 180°C.) for about 30 minutes with a lid on. When cooked, remove the lid and brown under a hot grill. Garnish with slices of hard-boiled egg.

# Burmese Cheese Rice

*An unusual combination of cheese with curry powder, but tasty and filling — another dish that is often popular with children, and always with adults.*

1 oz. (30 g.) butter

5 tomatoes, peeled and chopped

Salt and pepper

2 teaspoons curry powder (see page 174)

4 oz. (120 g.) grated cheese

8 oz. (250 g.) cooked rice

Toast triangles

Parsley

Paprika

Melt the butter in a heavy saucepan, add the tomatoes, salt, pepper and curry powder, and simmer for about 10 minutes. Stir in the cheese and the rice, heat through and make sure that the cheese has melted. Turn on to a hot serving dish, and garnish with the toast, parsley and a good sprinkling of paprika. Serve at once.

# Cauliflower Cheese and Bacon

*A favourite for lunch or dinner, particularly with children. Very economical, nourishing and easy to prepare.*

Wash and cut up the cauliflower and cook it in the usual way, being careful not to let it become over-cooked and soggy. In the meantime, grill the rashers, and prepare a cheese sauce:
Melt the butter and stir in the flour until smooth. Remove from the heat and gradually add the warmed milk, stirring all the time. When all the milk is added and the sauce is smooth, return to a very low heat and add the cheese, stirring until it has all melted. Season with pepper, but no salt. (There will already be sufficient salt from the cheese, and the cauliflower, which will have been cooked in salted water). Chop the grilled rashers, strain the cauliflower and carefully mix with the bacon. Put into a shallow fireproof dish, pour over the sauce, and garnish with the slices of tomato. Put under a hot grill for a few minutes so that it slightly browns. Serve very hot.

1 cauliflower
2 or 3 rashers
1 oz. (30 g.) butter
1 oz. (30 g.) flour
½ pint (300 ml.) milk
4 oz. (120 g.) grated cheese
1 large tomato, thinly sliced

# Simple Soufflé

*Another wartime recipe, very simple and quick to prepare.*

2 slices stale bread
1 egg
¾ – 1 pint (450 – 600 ml.) milk
4 – 6 oz. (120 – 180 g.) grated
   cheese
Butter
Salt, pepper, a pinch nutmeg

Butter the bread thinly and place one piece in the bottom of a greased pie-dish. Sprinkle in the grated cheese and place the other piece of bread on top. Beat the egg and mix it with the milk and seasonings. Pour over the contents of the dish and make sure that the milk soaks into the bread before cooking. Bake in a hot oven (Gas mark 8, Electric 450°F., 230°C.) for 20–30 minutes. Serve at once.

# Cheese and Sage Omelette

*An unusual variation on the ordinary cheese omelette. Sage was highly esteemed for its health-giving properties by the old herbalists — there was a proverb 'Why should a man die who has sage in his garden?' Try to use fresh sage if possible, but if you do have to use dried one teaspoon will be sufficient.*

4 oz. (120 g.) grated cheese

2 teaspoons sage

½ pint (300 ml.) milk

2 eggs

3 oz. (90 g.) fresh breadcrumbs

1 dessertspoon minced onion

Salt and pepper

Separate the eggs and beat the yolks. Warm the milk and add all the ingredients except the egg whites. Mix and allow to stand for one hour. Whip the egg whites stiffly and fold them into the mixture. Bake in a buttered fireproof dish (Gas mark 4, Electric 350°F., 180°C.) for 30 minutes.

# Celery and Cheese Flan

Shortcrust pastry case cooked 'blind'

1 onion

2 oz. (60 g.) butter

1 head cooked celery

1 oz. (30 g.) flour

½ pint (300 ml.) milk, or the water in which the celery was cooked

Salt and pepper

A little made mustard

2 oz. (60 g.) grated cheese

1 peeled tomato

Slice and chop the onion, melt 1 oz. (30 g.) butter in a frying-pan and fry the onion until golden brown. Chop the celery, add it to the onion, and heat gently. Make a white sauce with the rest of the butter, the flour and the liquid, and pour it over the vegetables. Add the seasoning, the mustard and most of the cheese. Pour the mixture into the pastry case, sprinkle with the rest of the cheese, and decorate with very thin slices of tomato. Heat and brown under a very hot grill, and serve straight away.

# Vegetable Pie with Cheese and Oatmeal Crust

*The Ministry of Food War Cookery Leaflet from which this recipe is adapted describes cheese as an A.1. food — it is an excellent body-builder, a concentrated energy-giving food, and a valuable protective food which helps to prevent certain forms of night blindness! And this is a splendid main meal dish which is very good served with jacket potatoes and a green vegetable.*

For the pie filling:
1½ lbs. (750 g.) cooked, mixed
    root vegetables
2 tablespoons chopped parsley
½ pint (300 ml.) stock or water
    (the water from the vegetables)

For the crust:
2 oz. (60 g.) oatmeal
2 oz. (60 g.) mashed potatoes
2 oz. (60 g.) grated cheese
Salt
4 oz. (120 g.) flour
1 oz. (30 g.) fat
Water to mix

Place the mixed vegetables in a pie dish and sprinkle with the parsley. Add the stock or water and seasoning.
To make the crust:
Cream the fat and the mashed potato together. Mix the cheese, oatmeal, flour and salt and stir this mixture into the creamed fat and potato. Mix to a stiff dough with the water. Roll out the dough on a floured board and cover the pie with it, trimming the edges neatly. Bake in a moderate oven (Gas mark 4, Electric 350ºF., 180ºC.) for about 30 minutes.

# Cheese and Lentil Rolls

*An interesting vegetarian recipe, which should be served very hot. These rolls make a very good dish for a buffet. Sufficient for six.*

Wash the lentils and tie them loosely in a piece of muslin in order to make them easier to handle later. Boil them for 1 hour in water, then rub them through a sieve. Add the butter, the skinned and chopped tomatoes, the cheese, salt, pepper and mustard, and

½ lb. (250 g.) puff pastry
1 cupful lentils
2 tomatoes
2 oz. (60 g.) grated cheese
1 cupful breadcrumbs
1 oz. (30 g.) butter
1 beaten egg
Salt and pepper
1 teaspoon dry mustard

enough breadcrumbs to make a thick mixture. Make sure that all the ingredients are thoroughly mixed in. Roll the pastry into a thin piece and cut it into small squares. Brush each with beaten egg and put a little roll of the lentil mixture in the centre of each. Fold the pastry over, as for a sausage roll, seal and trim the edge, brush with beaten egg, and place on a greased baking sheet, making sure that the rolls do not touch each other. Brush each roll with beaten egg and bake in a hot oven (Gas mark 8, Electric 450°F., 230°C.) for 20 minutes.

# La Truffado

*I first had this after it had been cooked over a log stove in a very primitive cottage in the South of France, and the potatoes were raw; I had it again cooked in the same cottage, but this time on a gas cooker, and it was delicious. In France they use Cantal cheese, but here we can use Cheshire — but make sure it is not processed, because then it will not melt.*

1 lb. (500 g.) potatoes
1 tablespoon butter
1 tablespoon oil
Salt and freshly ground black
    pepper
Pinch nutmeg
Handful diced bacon
1 clove garlic
2 oz. (60 g.) Cheshire cheese, cut
    into very small pieces

Peel the potatoes and slice them very thinly and evenly. Wash them in plenty of cold water. Heat the butter and oil in a thick frying pan, spread the potatoes evenly over the pan and add the bacon and finely chopped garlic. Season with salt and pepper and a pinch of nutmeg. As soon as the potatoes start to cook, turn the heat down, cover the pan and leave them to cook gently for about 15 minutes. By this time, the potatoes should have begun to coagulate into a pancake, and should be brown . underneath. Add the cheese, and turn the potatoes once or twice so that the cheese spreads all over them and both sides of the pancake are brown. Turn out onto a hot serving dish, and serve.

# Macaroni and Cheese Timbale

*For those who find macaroni cheese a bit dull. This dish looks very attractive garnished with quite a lot of fresh parsley.*

Cook the macaroni in boiling salted water in the usual way until soft. Drain well. In the meantime, prepare the cheese sauce:

Mix the flour to a smooth paste with a little of the cold milk. Boil the remainder of the liquid and stir it carefully into the paste. Return to the saucepan and boil for 3 minutes, stirring all the time. Add the seasoning and the butter, in small pieces. Add the butter a little at a time so that it does not become oily. Add the mustard, and stir in the cheese until it melts.

Turn the potatoes on to a floured board. Make them into a roll and put into a baking tin. Bank them up around the side of the tin to make a high ring and brush with beaten egg. Bake in a hot oven (Gas mark 7, Electric 425ºF., 220ºC.) for about 20 minutes, or until golden-brown. Carefully remove from the tin and place on the serving dish. Fill the centre with the macaroni and cheese sauce well mixed together and serve garnished with plenty of parsley.

1½ lb. (750 g.) cooked mashed
   potatoes
2 oz. (60 g.) macaroni
For the cheese sauce:
½ oz. (15 g.) butter
½ oz. (15 g.) flour
½ pint (300 ml.) milk
1 oz. (30 g.) grated cheese
1 teaspoon made mustard
Salt and pepper
Parsley

# Potato Latkes

*A Jewish dish, very tasty, and substantial enough to be served simply with sliced garlic sausage and gherkins.*

Peel the potatoes and soak them in cold water for about 1 hour. Grate them, and allow them to drain thoroughly. Stir in the beaten eggs, flour, chopped onion, salt and pepper. Heat the oil in a frying pan, and drop in spoonfuls of the mixture, cooking them well on both sides.

4 potatoes
2 oz. (60 g.) flour
1 tablespoon chopped onion
2 eggs
Salt and pepper
Oil or fat for frying

# Gnocchi

*An Italian dish for which it is best to use Parmesan cheese, although Cheddar can be used if Parmesan is not available. It can be eaten on its own or with a meat dish.*

½ oz. (15 g.) butter

½ pint (300 ml.) milk

2 oz. (60 g.) semolina

Salt and pepper

1 yolk of egg

4 tablespoons thick white sauce

3 oz. (90 g.) grated Parmesan
    cheese

Add the butter to the milk and bring to the boil. When boiling, sprinkle in the semolina and simmer until it is thoroughly cooked and the mixture is thick. Remove from the heat, add the salt and pepper and the egg yolk, and beat together to mix thoroughly. Turn the mixture onto a plate, smooth it and leave to become completely cold. When cold, cut it into even squares. Heat the white sauce, add most of the cheese to it, put the gnocchi in the bottom of a shallow fireproof dish and pour over the sauce. Sprinkle with the rest of the cheese and brown in a hot oven (Gas mark 7, Electric 425°F., 220°C.) for about 8 minutes, so that the cheese has melted and slightly browned.

# American Cheese Dish

*A recommended protein dish in a wartime recipe book, which sounds rather dull — in fact it is very tasty served as a sauce with green vegetables.*

1 teaspoon finely chopped onion
    (or leeks or chives)

1 tomato, skinned and reduced to
    pulp in a very little butter

½ tablespoon very finely chopped
    green pepper

4 oz. (120 g.) grated cheese

2 – 4 tablespoons milk

1 beaten egg

Melt a little fat in a saucepan, add the onion, tomato, pepper, cheese, milk and egg. Stir until the mixture thickens and season to taste. Serve very hot on green vegetables.

# Egg and Bacon Tart

*An economical version of the proper quiche lorraine, this is very cheap and easy to make. It can be a first course or a main dish, which is particularly good for summer lunch, accompanied by a really crisp salad.*

Shortcrust pastry case (baked
    blind — i.e. lined with paper
    and filled with beans or
    something similar)
1 egg
1 egg yolk
2 oz. (60 g.) grated cheese
About ¼ pint (150 ml.) milk
1 small onion
1 tomato
2 oz. (60 g.) bacon
Salt, pepper and nutmeg
Butter

Beat the eggs and cheese together in a bowl and add the milk and seasoning. Chop the onion and bacon into small pieces and fry them gently in a little butter for about 5 minutes. Sprinkle this all over the bottom of the pastry case. Slice the tomato and arrange the slices in the pastry case. Pour over the egg mixture. Bake in a moderate oven (Gas mark 5, 370°F., 190°C.) for about 45 minutes.

# Cheese Pudding

*A pudding with a most appetising smell and appearance. Ideal for a cold winter day.*

1 pint (600 ml.) milk
3 oz. (90 g.) breadcrumbs
1 egg
Salt and pepper
1 teaspoon freshly made mustard
3 oz. (90 g.) finely grated cheese
Parsley

Heat the milk and pour it over the breadcrumbs, leave to soak for about ¼ hour, then beat well with a fork. Separate the egg, and add it to the bread-crumbs with the salt, pepper, mustard and three quarters of the cheese. Whisk the egg white stiffly and fold it into the mixture lightly. Grease a pie dish and fill it with the mixture. Sprinkle with the rest of the cheese and bake in a moderately hot oven (Gas mark 6, Electric 400°F., 200°C.) until golden and well risen — between 30 and 40 minutes.

# Savoury Cheese Pie

*A good main course accompanied by potatoes and green vegetables.*

8 oz. (250 g.) shortcrust pastry
4 oz. (120 g.) boiled ham
2 tomatoes
4 oz. (120 g.) Cheddar cheese,
   cut into thin slices
1 egg
¼ pint (150 ml.) milk

Roll out the pastry thinly and line a 7 in. x 2 in. pie dish, using about two thirds of it. Press it well down and prick all over. Put a layer of ham in the dish, cover with sliced tomatoes, sprinkle with salt and pepper, then cover with the slices of cheese. Beat the egg, mix it with the milk, season with salt and pepper, and pour over the cheese. Make a lid from the remaining pastry, moisten the edges and cover the pie. Decorate the top with trimmings made from the leftover bits of pastry. Brush with a little milk and bake in a fairly hot oven (Gas mark 7, Electric 425°F., 220°C.) for about half an hour, or until the pastry is well-browned.

# Eggs Benedictine

*A substantial dish, adequate for a main course. You can use any white fish (cod, haddock, coley or whiting).*

4 soft-boiled eggs (boiled for five
   minutes and then plunged in
   cold water)
12 oz. (360 g.) cooked white
   fish
½ oz. (15 g.) butter
1 clove garlic
¼ pint (150 ml.) white sauce
2 tablespoons top of the milk
½ pint (300 ml.) cheese sauce
   (white sauce with grated
   cheese stirred in)
2 tablespoons grated cheese

Shell the eggs carefully without breaking them, and put them in a bowl of warm water until you need them. Melt the butter in a saucepan and cook the crushed garlic in it for a minute before adding the flaked fish. Stir and add the white sauce. Stir thoroughly over a low heat and when well mixed stir in the milk. Spread this mixture evenly in a buttered fireproof dish. Cut the eggs in half (remember that the yolks are soft), and arrange them, yolk uppermost on top of the fish mixture. Pour over the cheese sauce, sprinkle with grated cheese, and brown lightly under the grill. If you wish, you can leave the eggs whole.

# Lettuce and Egg

*A delicate and subtle dish which is very simple to prepare. It should be served sizzling hot and bubbling, with triangles of thin dry toast arranged around the edge of the dish. It looks very attractive served in individual soufflé dishes, but can equally well be served in a shallow fireproof dish.*

To prepare the béchamel:
Heat the milk to simmering point in a heavy saucepan. Pour the milk into a jug and rinse out the pan. Put in the butter and when it is hot, but has not changed colour, take the pan from the heat and stir in the flour with a wooden spoon. In a few seconds you will have a thick smooth paste. Still keeping the pan away from the heat, start adding the hot milk, a little at a time. Stir constantly as each small quantity of milk is added so that the paste is always smooth, and, when about half the milk is added, return the pan to a very low heat, preferably on an asbestos mat. Continue adding the milk and stirring until you have a thin smooth cream. It should then be seasoned with about half a teaspoon of salt, a quarter teaspoon freshly ground black pepper and a generous pinch of nutmeg. Cook very gently for about 15 minutes.

Wash, drain and cut the lettuce into thin strips. Melt the butter in a saucepan and cook the lettuce for about 10 minutes over a low heat. Season with salt and a pinch of sugar. Stir this mixture into the prepared béchamel. Shell the eggs and cut them into quarters, add them to the lettuce sauce and stir in the cream very gently, so as not to break up the eggs. Put the whole into a shallow fireproof dish, sprinkle with breadcrumbs and dot with butter. Put into a moderately hot oven (Gas mark 5, Electric 375°F., 190°C.) for about 10 minutes.

1 large lettuce weighing approx.
½ lb. (250 g.) either cos or cabbage variety
4 hard-boiled eggs
¼ pint (150 ml.) cream
4 tablespoons breadcrumbs
1 oz. (30 g.) butter
Béchamel made from:
1 oz. (30 g.) butter
1 tablespoon flour
½ pint (300 ml.) milk
Salt, pepper and nutmeg

# Spanish Eggs

*A dish to make when the vegetables are plentiful and cheap. It is worth using asparagus if you possibly can, but it is not essential. The food value is high, and there is no need to serve anything with this dish as it already contains vegetables in quantity. The quantities given here will provide a substantial meal for four, and it can be stretched to feed more by simply increasing the number of eggs and the quantity of vegetables.*

1 or 2 eggs per person
1 large onion
2 cloves garlic
1 lb. (500 g.) peas
1 lb. (500 g.) green beans
1 small tin red peppers
4 large ripe tomatoes
1 small tin asparagus
2 rashers streaky bacon
4 slices ham (or ham-cured
    shoulder — cheaper)
¼ lb. (120 g.) garlic sausage
Salt and pepper
Oil (olive, preferably)

Heat the oil in a large saucepan and gently fry the chopped onion and garlic for about five minutes. Chop the rashers and tomatoes and stir them into the onion mixture. Cook gently for about 10 minutes. Pod the peas and slice the beans, stir them in to the pan and season with salt and freshly ground black pepper. Add water to cover, stir thoroughly and cook with the lid on for about 15 minutes. Chop half the peppers from the tin and add to the mixture together with the asparagus. Allow to heat through. Transfer the whole to a shallow fireproof dish, and cover the surface with the ham and sliced garlic sausage (from which you have removed the skin). You can cut the garlic sausage into strips and use them to mark out the spaces into which you will break the eggs. Break the eggs onto the surface. Put the dish into the bottom of a very hot oven (Gas mark 9, Electric 475°F., 240°C.) for about 10 minutes to set the eggs. Serve very hot, garnished with the remainder of the peppers, cut into strips.

# Eggs in Snail Butter

*Really good, as long as you like garlic. The number of eggs you use depends entirely on you, but if you provide one per person, then obviously the dish is more suitable for an hors d'oeuvre.*

Eggs
2 oz. (60 g.) butter
2 cloves garlic
1 shallot
A little salt
Freshly ground black pepper
Parsley

Pound the butter with the garlic, shallot, salt, pepper and parsley. Cook the eggs in a little butter in fire-proof egg-dishes, if you have them — if not, you can put them all into a flat fireproof dish in which you have already melted the butter. Cook them over a gentle heat, so that the whites do not go brown at the edges. Just before they are cooked, put a little of the snail butter on top of each. Serve immediately.

# Arabian Eggs

*An unusual Middle Eastern recipe which can be served with Savoury rice (p. 172) or plain boiled rice. Enough for six people.*

6 eggs
2 oz. (60 g.) butter
½ teaspoon each of salt, paprika,
    black pepper, cinnamon

Mix the spices together thoroughly. Melt the butter in a shallow pan. Hard boil the eggs and shell them while still warm. Prick the whites all over and cook them gently in the butter turning them over and over until light brown. Place on a warm serving dish and sprinkle with the salt and the spices.

# Fish

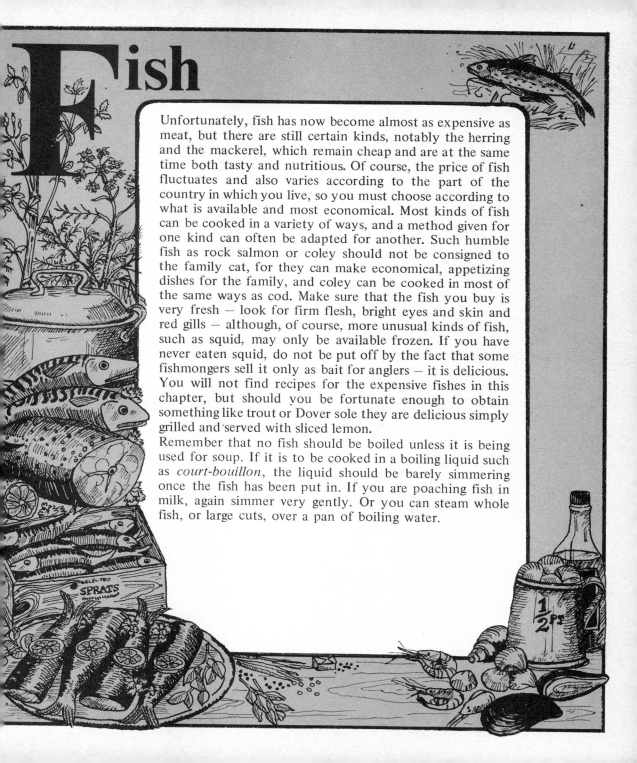

Unfortunately, fish has now become almost as expensive as meat, but there are still certain kinds, notably the herring and the mackerel, which remain cheap and are at the same time both tasty and nutritious. Of course, the price of fish fluctuates and also varies according to the part of the country in which you live, so you must choose according to what is available and most economical. Most kinds of fish can be cooked in a variety of ways, and a method given for one kind can often be adapted for another. Such humble fish as rock salmon or coley should not be consigned to the family cat, for they can make economical, appetizing dishes for the family, and coley can be cooked in most of the same ways as cod. Make sure that the fish you buy is very fresh — look for firm flesh, bright eyes and skin and red gills — although, of course, more unusual kinds of fish, such as squid, may only be available frozen. If you have never eaten squid, do not be put off by the fact that some fishmongers sell it only as bait for anglers — it is delicious. You will not find recipes for the expensive fishes in this chapter, but should you be fortunate enough to obtain something like trout or Dover sole they are delicious simply grilled and served with sliced lemon.

Remember that no fish should be boiled unless it is being used for soup. If it is to be cooked in a boiling liquid such as *court-bouillon*, the liquid should be barely simmering once the fish has been put in. If you are poaching fish in milk, again simmer very gently. Or you can steam whole fish, or large cuts, over a pan of boiling water.

# Fried Herrings in Oatmeal

*The classic Scottish method of cooking herrings which can scarcely be improved upon. You can grill or fry the herrings; remember that they are an oily fish so that very little oil or fat is required.*

Clean and fillet the herrings, split them and cut off the fins. Spread them flat and coat them all over with medium oatmeal. Heat a very little oil in a frying pan and fry the herrings gently until golden brown. Drain them very well before serving them garnished with parsley. Mustard sauce, for which two recipes will be found on p. 51, goes very well with this dish.

# Herrings à la Portière

*This is best if really fresh herrings are used. Sprats may be cooked in this way, but there is no need to clean or score them.*

1 medium-sized herring per person
A little milk
A little made mustard (freshly-made English or Dijon)
Seasoned flour
2 oz. (60 g.) butter
1 dessertspoon chopped parsley
1 tablespoon wine vinegar, or a small glass white wine

Remove the heads and clean the herrings, but do not fillet them unless a member of the family objects strongly to bones. Score them lightly two or three times on each side. Dip them in milk, roll them in the seasoned flour and fry them gently in two thirds of the butter. When cooked, arrange them on a dish and brush them on both sides with a little mustard. Sprinkle them with parsley and keep hot. Melt the rest of the butter in the pan in which the herrings were cooked and pour it over them. Turn off the heat and swill out the pan with the wine vinegar or wine and pour that over the fish. Serve at once.

# Grilled Herrings with Mustard Sauce

*Another herring classic which can also be used for mackerel. Two versions of the sauce are given, the first for special occasions, the second more economical.*

1 herring per person
A little oil

Grill the cleaned and filleted herrings, using very little oil. Meanwhile, prepare the sauce:

For the sauce (1):
2 teaspoons yellow Dijon
    mustard (or freshly made
    English mustard)
1 tablespoon chopped parsley
3 oz. (90 g.) butter
Good squeeze lemon juice

(1) Put the mustard into a bowl and stir in the parsley and then the barely melted butter. Stir until completely smooth and then add the lemon juice. This sauce can be varied by the addition of other herbs — chervil or fennel are particularly good.

For the sauce (2):
1 tablespoon dry mustard
½ tablespoon flour
1 teaspoon vinegar
Approx. ¼ pint (150 ml.) water
1 oz. (30 g.) butter
Salt and pepper

(2) Melt the butter in a double saucepan and stir in all the other ingredients until smooth and thick. If too thick add a little more water. A few chopped capers are a good addition to this sauce.

# Herrings Stuffed with Onion

*Very simple to prepare, but really delicious.*

2 herrings per person (unless
    they are very large)
1 medium onion for each herring
Oil for frying the onion

Slice the onions into neat rings and fry them until they are crisp and golden. Have the herrings cleaned and filleted (the fishmonger will usually do this for you, if you ask), and stuff each one with the onion rings. Grill quickly, and serve at once.

# Grandma's Soused Herrings

*Sprats or mackerel may be treated in the same way, and may be served hot, garnished with slices of lemon and gherkins, or cold, as an hors d'oeuvre, or with salad.*

2 small herrings per person
4 cloves
2 dried red chillies
1 blade mace, or a pinch nutmeg
12 black peppercorns
1 teaspoon salt
2 bayleaves
1 teacup wine vinegar
1 teacup water

Cut off the heads and tails and clean the herrings without splitting them. Arrange them in a shallow fireproof dish and all the other ingredients. Bake in a moderate oven (Gas mark 4, Electric 350°F., 180°C.) for about ¾ hour. If they are to be served cold, allow them to cool in the pickle.

# Herrings Boulangère

*A French method of cooking herrings which is very good served with spinach or kale.*

1 large or 2 small herrings per
   person
1 large potato
1 large onion
1 teaspoon dried thyme
1 teaspoon powdered bayleaf
Salt and pepper
3 oz. (90 g.) butter

Remove the heads and clean the herrings without splitting them. Butter a shallow ovenproof dish and arrange the herrings in a row, leaving a space at the sides of the dish. Sprinkle them with salt, pepper and herbs. Slice the vegetables very thinly and arrange them round the fish. Melt the butter and pour it over the fish and vegetables, then add enough cold water to barely cover. Bring to the boil and then transfer to a fairly hot oven (Gas mark 5, Electric 375°F., 190°C.) and cook for about 45 minutes, basting occasionally.

# Mackerel Lyonnaise

*As mackerel is a strongly flavoured fish onions go very well with them. This dish is good served with jacket potatoes and spinach.*

2 large mackerel
2 large onions
2 tablespoons wine vinegar
2 oz. (60 g.) butter
Salt and pepper
Breadcrumbs
3 tablespoons cider or white
    wine

Clean and fillet the mackerel or ask the fishmonger to do it for you. Peel and slice the onions thinly and melt 1½ oz. (45 g.) butter in a pan. Stew the onions very slowly until they are soft and then stir in the vinegar. Spread half the onion on the bottom of a flat ovenproof dish and lay the fillets on top. Sprinkle with salt and pepper. Cover with the rest of the onions. Pour over the cider or wine, sprinkle with breadcrumbs, and dot with the remaining butter. Bake in a fairly hot oven until the fillets are tender (Gas mark 5, Electric 375°F., 190°C.) — usually about 25 minutes.

# Fillets of Mackerel with Capers

*Ask the fishmonger to fillet the mackerel for you, unless you are an expert — but do ask him for the bones, which should be used to make stock.*

1 mackerel per person (depending
    on size — they are sometimes
    very big)
¼ pint (150 ml.) stock, made from
    the bones
Small glass white wine or dry cider
½ oz. (15 g.) butter
1 dessertspoon flour
1 egg
1 tablespoon capers
Breadcrumbs, salt and pepper

Arrange the fillets in a shallow buttered fireproof dish, sprinkle with salt and pepper and pour over the wine or cider. Cover them and bake in a moderate oven (Gas mark 4, Electric 350°F., 180°C.) for about 30 minutes. Meanwhile, melt the butter in a saucepan and stir in the flour; after a minute, stir in the stock until smooth and creamy. Beat the egg and stir into the sauce, but do not let it boil. Stir in the capers and pour over the mackerel. Sprinkle with breadcrumbs, and a very little melted butter and brown under the grill. Be careful not to leave it under the grill for more than about 3 minutes or the sauce may curdle.

# Fillets of Mackerel with Fresh Tomato Sauce and Potatoes

*This is perfectly adequate for a main course, and can be followed by a green salad.*

**1 large mackerel per person**
**Seasoned flour**
**1 oz. (30 g.) butter**
**Hot boiled potatoes**
**1 tablespoon olive oil**
**Salt and pepper**
**A little vinegar**

**For the tomato sauce:**
**1 lb. (500 g.) ripe tomatoes**
**1 tablespoon olive oil**
**1 small onion**
**1 clove garlic**
**1 carrot**
**Some parsley stalks**
**A little fresh or dried marjoram**
**    or basil**
**A little salt and freshly ground**
**    black pepper.**

Clean and fillet the mackerel and coat lightly with seasoned flour. Fry them in the melted butter. Slice the potatoes and season them with olive oil, salt and pepper and a little vinegar. Arrange them in a circle on the serving dish with the fried fillets.

To make the sauce:
Chop the tomatoes and put them in a thick saucepan with the olive oil, the chopped onion, the crushed garlic, the chopped carrot, parsley, marjoram or basil and salt and pepper. Simmer until the tomatoes are a thick pulp, check the seasoning, sieve if desired, and serve with the mackerel in a separate bowl.

# Stuffed Mackerel

*A little more fiddly then the preceding recipes, but well worth the effort. It produces a very substantial meal when accompanied by boiled potatoes and a green vegetable.*

2 medium-sized mackerel

3 tablespoons breadcrumbs

1 dessertspoon chopped parsley

1 dessertspoon chopped capers
    or gherkins

5 mushrooms

A little grated lemon rind

2 oz. (60 g.) butter

A little milk

Salt and pepper

Clean and fillet the fish, leaving the tails on. Put the breadcrumbs into a bowl with the parsley, capers or gherkins, chopped mushrooms, lemon rind, pepper and salt. Melt the butter and add half to the stuffing with enough milk to moisten it. Put this stuffing on one side of each fillet, fold them over and sew them up carefully with a needle and strong cotton so that the stuffing is completely contained. Place the fish in a fireproof dish, pour the remaining butter over them, cover with a piece of foil, and bake in a moderate oven (Gas mark 4, Electric 350ºF., 180ºF.) for about ½ hour. When they are cooked, remove the cotton carefully and serve. The tomato sauce given for the previous recipe may also be served with this dish.

# Spiced Mackerel

*An old English way of cooking mackerel. Goose-berry sauce goes very well with this, and boiled new potatoes or green salad.*

4 medium-sized mackerel

Salt

Slices of orange or lemon

6 bayleaves

1 teaspoon allspice berries or
    black peppercorns

A few parsley stalks

3 or 4 dried fennel stalks

3 tablespoons wine vinegar

½ pint (300 ml.) water

Clean the mackerel but do not split them and sprinkle them, inside and out, with salt. Arrange them in a shallow baking tin and add the orange or lemon, the bay leaves, allspice or peppercorns, parsley stalks and fennel. Pour over the vinegar and water. Cover the tin with foil and bake in the centre of a moderate oven (Gas mark 4, Electric 350ºF., 180ºC.) for about 30 minutes.

# Fillets of Mackerel in White Wine

*This dish is often served as an hors d'oeuvre, but, accompanied by mustard sauce (see recipe under Grilled Herrings, Sauce (1), with fennel or chervil, p.51), it makes an excellent cold main course, followed by green salad.*

1 mackerel per person

A few capers

1 teaspoon chopped chives or
    parsley

For the court-bouillon:

1 wineglass white wine

1 wineglass water

1 onion

1 clove garlic

1 bayleaf

Salt and black pepper

1 piece of lemon peel

Clean the mackerel but do not fillet them. Prepare the *court-bouillon*:
Put all the ingredients into a saucepan and bring to the boil, letting it cook for 5 minutes, then leave it to cool.
Put the mackerel into the cold *court-bouillon*, making sure the pan is large enough to avoid bending them. Bring to the boil and simmer very gently for about ¼ hour. Leave them to get cold in the *court-bouillon*. Split the fish very carefully, take out the bones and remove the skin. Divide the fish into several small fillets and arrange them in a suitable dish. Reheat the *court-bouillon* and let it bubble until it is reduced by half, then allow it to cool, and strain it over the fish. Serve garnished with capers and chives or parsley.

# Coley or Cod

Note that all recipes given for coley may be used for cod, and vice-versa. Although coley may have a rather unprepossessing appearance when raw, it goes white when it is cooked. It is sold both in steaks and fillets. If you see cod cheek it is well worth buying — it is half the price of cod, there is no waste, and it is very good dipped in seasoned flour, fried, and served with fresh lemon.

# Spiced Fillet of Coley

*Try to get the fish in one piece for this dish. You can use saithe, cod or haddock as an alternative, depending on what is available and cheapest.*

2 lb. (1 kg.) coley
½ teaspoon mixed spice
¼ teaspoon ground ginger
½ teaspoon salt
1 pinch cayenne
1 pinch caraway seeds
1 dessertspoon brown sugar
Grated rind and juice of half a
    lemon
1½ oz. (45 g.) butter
1 clove garlic (crushed or chopped
    very finely)
1 teaspoon ground coriander

Cream two thirds of the butter partially, then add the mixed spice, ginger, salt, coriander, caraway seeds, sugar, lemon rind, and garlic. Cream again. Skin the fish and spread the skinned side with the unflavoured butter. Salt lightly and sprinkle with a little lemon juice. Place in a shallow fireproof dish and place under a hot grill for about 5 minutes. Turn the fish over and sprinkle the uncooked side with salt and lemon juice. Then spread with the flavoured (spiced) butter. Grill for 8 minutes, basting with the juices in the dish. Serve accompanied with plain boiled rice, or with small boiled potatoes, fried onions or grilled tomatoes.

# Coley in Cider

*Once again, cod can be used in this recipe – or, if you want to be really extravagant, plaice.*

½ lb. (250 g.) filleted coley for
    each person
1 tablespoon olive oil
1 pint (600 ml.) dry cider
1 oz. (40 g.) butter
1 oz. (30 g.) flour
1 dessertspoon chopped parsley
1 medium-sized chopped onion
¼ lb. (120 g.) chopped mushrooms
Salt and pepper

Put the fillets in a casserole with the olive oil and the cider. Melt the butter in a saucepan and stir in the flour, parsley, onion and mushrooms. Spread this mixture over the fillets, cover and bake in a moderate oven for ½ hour (Gas mark 4, Electric 350ºF., 180ºC.).

# Casserole of Cod

*A substantial dish, requiring only a green salad to follow.*

4 cod cutlets or fillets
½ lb. (250 g.) tomatoes
3 sliced carrots
1 large sliced onion
1 chopped celery stalk
1 lb. (500 g.) potatoes
2 oz. (60 g.) butter
Fat or oil for frying
¼ pint (150 ml.) milk
Salt and pepper
Chopped parsley

Wash the fish, removing any fins. Slice the tomatoes. Heat the oil in a frying pan, and fry the carrots, onion and celery lightly. Remove them from the pan and keep them hot. Grease a casserole, and put half the tomatoes in a layer at the bottom. Add the fried vegetables and sprinkle with salt and pepper. Put the fish on top and cover with the remaining tomatoes. Sprinkle with salt and pepper (a little dried marjoram may be sprinkled on at this stage, if desired). Peel and slice the potatoes thinly and spread them all over the top of the dish. Dot with butter and pour on the milk. Cover the dish and bake at Gas mark 6 (Electric 400°F., 200°C.) for about 1 hour, removing the lid for the last 15 minutes to allow the potatoes to brown.

# Cod with Anchovies

*Originally a Spanish recipe, which can be made equally well with coley or haddock. It is very good accompanied with left-over boiled potatoes, sliced, mixed with a little finely chopped garlic, and sautéed.*

½ lb. (250 g.) fillet for each
    person
1 small tin flat fillets of anchovies
1 slice of white bread for each
    piece of fish (the same size as
    the fish)
Tomato sauce (see recipe on
    page 54)
A little melted butter
Oil for frying the bread

Brush each fillet with a little melted butter and grill. Fry the bread, and place 2 or 3 anchovies on each piece. Place the cooked fish on top, and pour tomato sauce over.

# Baked Sprats

*Sprats are very tasty and cheap in season. They require a minimum of preparation, only washing, and the heads and tails can be left on or not according to personal preference. The easiest way to cook them is to dip them in seasoned flour and either deep or shallow frying. They should then be well drained and served with slices of lemon, and a sprinkling of chopped parsley. The two recipes following take longer but are well worth the effort.*

Grease a round baking tin. Wash the sprats, and arrange them, one deep, in a circle with their tails in the middle. Sprinkle with salt and pepper, a squeeze of lemon juice, a sprinkling of chopped parsley, and a thin layer of tomato purée. Then put in another layer of sprats and continue with alternate layers of sprats and the other ingredients until the tin is full, finishing with salt, pepper, lemon juice, parsley and tomato purée. Dot with butter, and sprinkle on more parsley, cover with a piece of foil and bake in a moderate oven (Gas mark 4, Electric 350ºF., 180ºC.), for ¾ − 1 hour, removing the foil for the last 10 minutes.

2 lb. (1 kg.) sprats
Lemon juice
A handful of parsley
Tomato purée (either home-
    made, or a small tin)
Salt and pepper
Butter

# Potted Sprats

*This is a more spicy way of cooking sprats, and similar to the method given for spiced mackerel.*

Wash the sprats and remove their heads and tails. Dry them and arrange them in a shallow fireproof dish. Sprinkle with salt and pepper, and add all the other ingredients except the butter which should be dotted all over the top. Cover with foil and bake in a moderate oven (Gas mark 4, Electric 350ºF., 180ºC.) for 20 − 30 minutes.

½ lb. (250 g.) sprats per person
Salt and pepper
2 bayleaves
1 blade mace
1 medium chopped onion
Pinch nutmeg
1 cup of wine vinegar, and 1 of
    water
Butter

# Baked Conger Eel

*Conger eel is usually cheap, but tends to be a bit bony — if you have a friendly fishmonger you can ask him to give you the least bony section, which tends to be towards the head end of the eel. It has a very good flavour, and will provide a substantial meal. The quantities given below will certainly serve six people.*

3 lb. (1.5 kg.) conger eel
2 tablespoons wine vinegar
1 dessertspoon chopped onion
Pepper and salt
2 or 3 anchovy fillets
2 oz. (60 g.) butter
A little flour
½ pint (300 ml.) white sauce
    (see page 177)
1 dessertspoon anchovy essence

For the stuffing:
3 tablespoons breadcrumbs
1 dessertspoon chopped parsley
Grated rind of half a lemon
½ teaspoon mixed dried herbs
1 teaspoon anchovy essence
1 tablespoon melted butter
Salt and pepper
Milk to bind

To make the stuffing:
Put the breadcrumbs and seasonings into a basin, add the butter and bind with the milk.

Wash and dry the eel and let it stand for about 1 hour in a marinade made with the vinegar, onion, pepper and salt, turning it occasionally. Chop the anchovies and stir them into the prepared stuffing. Cut into the eel in several places, into the bone, put in the stuffing close to the bone and tie the fish up with string or tape. Lay the fish in a greased baking tin, dredge it with flour, and dot with the butter in small pieces. Bake in a moderate oven (Gas mark 4, Electric 350°F., 180°C.) for about 1½ hours, or until tender. Place the fish on a hot dish, and remove the string. Heat the white sauce, stir in the anchovy essence, and strain it over the eel. Serve very hot, garnished with parsley and lemon. Sauté potatoes and green vegetables make a good accompaniment for this impressive dish.

# Conger Eel Sautéed with Capers

*Allow one steak about 1½ inches thick per person — ask the fishmonger to cut them for you. This dish is very quick to prepare, and it can be served in the middle of creamy mashed potatoes.*

1 conger eel steak per person
Butter or oil for sautéing
1 dessertspoon flour
1 tablespoon capers

Wash the eel and remove any fins. Sauté gently in the butter or oil. When cooked, remove carefully from the pan, and keep hot. Stir the flour into the pan, and add the capers. Arrange the fish on a bed of mashed potatoes, and pour the sauce over.

# Rock Salmon à la Meunière

*A very cheap fish and very good cooked in this simple, classic fashion. This recipe is a wartime one, said to have been used by a famous Paris restaurant, as a substitute for the more expensive fish which were often unobtainable.*

1 cutlet per person
Seasoned flour
Butter for frying
A squeeze of lemon juice
Chopped parsley
Garnish of sliced gherkins, capers
    or small grilled tomatoes

Coat the cutlets in seasoned flour and fry them in butter till golden-brown. For the real *meunière,* you should then discard the butter in which the fish was fried, clean your pan, melt 2 oz. (60 g.) fresh butter, and when it is foaming pour it over the fish. However, in the interests of economy, you can use the butter in which you cooked the fish. Dust the fish with finely chopped parsley and garnish with gherkins, capers or small grilled tomatoes, add a squeeze of lemon juice and serve.

# Whiting Soufflé

*Although this requires two eggs, it uses very little of anything else, and can be served as a main course, if preceded by a filling soup, and followed by a green salad.*

4 oz. (120 g.) cooked whiting (minus skin and bone)

1 oz. (30 g.) butter

½ oz. (15 g.) flour

¼ pint (150 ml.) milk (or fish stock, which can be made from the bones)

Lemon peel

Anchovy essence

Salt and pepper

1 oz. (30 g.) breadcrumbs

2 eggs

1 or 2 tablespoons cream (optional)

Pound the fish to a paste. Melt the butter in a saucepan, add the flour and cook for a minute, stirring. Stir in the milk or stock and bring to the boil, making a smooth sauce. Cook for a few minutes, stirring all the time. Add salt, pepper, lemon peel, anchovy essence, fish, breadcrumbs, and cream (for which top of the milk may be substituted). Mix well. Separate the eggs, beat the yolks and whip the whites stiffly. Beat the yolks into the mixture, and stir in the whites very lightly. Put into a greased soufflé dish and bake for 25 minutes as Gas mark 6, Electric 400°F., 200°C.

# Whiting with Mushrooms

*If you can get large whiting, this dish will serve six people, particularly if it follows a fairly substantial hors d'oeuvre.*

Clean and fillet the whiting (they can also be skinned, but this is not essential) and divide each fish into two fillets. Season with salt and pepper. Wash, peel and chop the mushrooms, including the stalks. Melt about 1 oz. (30 g.) butter in a small

4 whiting
Butter
Oil
Salt and pepper
A little flour
¼ lb. (120 g.) mushrooms
2 tablespoons chopped onion
1 teaspoon chopped parsley
2 tablespoons breadcrumbs

pan and cook the onion for a few minutes. Then add the mushrooms and season with salt and pepper and cook for about 8 minutes. Stir in the parsley. Coat the fillets lightly with flour and fry them in the oil until cooked and golden brown. Spread the mushroom mixture in the bottom of a greased fireproof dish and arrange the fish on top. Sprinkle with breadcrumbs and pour over a little melted butter. Brown quickly under a hot grill and serve at once, garnished with parsley and sliced lemon.

# Russian Whiting

2 or 3 whiting
3 young carrots
1 small onion
1 tablespoon parsley (not
    chopped, but left in small
    sprigs)
¼ pint (150 ml.) water
1 glass white wine
½ oz. (15 g.) butter (or ¼ oz.
    (10 g.) butter and 1 dessert-
    spoon sour cream)
Salt and pepper

*To make this a little more authentic, sour cream may be substituted for the butter which is added at the end of this recipe. Spinach is a good accompaniment, or green peas.*

Slice the onion and carrot very thinly and put in a small saucepan with the water, ¼ oz. (10 g.) butter and the parsley. Add a little salt and cook for a few minutes until the vegetables are tender. Meanwhile, clean the whiting without splitting them and put them in a greased ovenproof dish. Pour over the wine, and the vegetables and liquid. Bake in a moderate oven (Gas mark 4, 350°F., 180°C.) for about ½ hour. Lift the fish carefully into the serving dish and reduce the liquid by about half by fast boiling. Stir in the remaining butter or sour cream at the last minute and do not allow to boil. Pour all over the fish and serve at once.

# Fish Timbale

*There are several recipes for Fish Timbale, some simpler than others but this particular version has been included because it makes a very good main course, requiring only green vegetables, or even salad as an accompaniment.*

Boil the potatoes and mash them thoroughly, seasoning with salt and pepper and nutmeg. Separate the egg and beat the yolk into the potatoes. Grease a soufflé dish, or other straight-sided oven proof dish, and sprinkle it with breadcrumbs. Pack in the mashed potatoes and bake them at Gas mark 3, Electric 325°F., 170°C. for 40 minutes. Remove from the oven and very carefully cut the top off the potatoes in one piece about an inch thick, being careful not to break it. Then scoop out the potatoes leaving a wall at the sides and at bottom about one inch thick. Paint the inner surface with the white of egg and return it to the oven for a few minutes to dry the egg white. Make a thick white sauce with the flour, butter and milk, season it with the salt and pepper, and stir in the anchovy essence, the flaked fish, and the chopped mushrooms. Mix thoroughly and allow to cook for about 5 minutes, stirring all the time. Pour this mixture into the potato case and replace the lid, pressing it down carefully but firmly. If you then leave it to stand for a few seconds you should be able to turn the timbale out onto a serving dish without breaking it. Garnish it with some good sprigs of parsley and serve.

1½ lb. (750 g.) potatoes
Salt and pepper
Pinch nutmeg
1 egg
Breadcrumbs
1 oz. (30 g.) flour
1 oz. (30 g.) butter
¼ pint (150 ml.) milk
Salt and pepper
1 teaspoon anchovy essence
Any cooked white fish
¼ lb. (120 g.) chopped mushrooms

# Paprika Fish

*A dish which is very quickly prepared and good
made with almost any kind of fish — Finnan
haddock is often recommended, but unsmoked
fish such as coley, cod or haddock are also very
good — it can even be made with kipper fillets, but
these do tend to overcome the cheese flavour a bit.*

1 lb. (500 g.) fish
1 lb. (500 g.) noodles (see page
   36), or macaroni, or any other
   pasta
1 oz. (30 g.) butter
1 oz. (30 g.) flour
¼ — ½ pint (150 — 300 ml.) milk
6 oz. (180 g.) grated cheese
Black pepper
Paprika

Steam the fish. Cook the noodles in fast-boiling
salted water. Meanwhile, make a white sauce with
the flour, butter and milk, and stir in 4 oz. (120 g.)
of the cheese. Add pepper, but no salt or the
finished dish will be far too salty. Strain the
noodles and flake the fish, and mix the two together carefully. Then stir in the cheese sauce and
put the whole into a greased fireproof dish. This
should all be done very quickly so that all ingredients remain hot. Sprinkle the remaining cheese all
over the top, and add a good sprinkling of paprika.
Put under a hot grill until the cheese is golden and
bubbling.

# Fresh-water Fish

I have recently noticed a number of fishmongers are
starting to offer a variety of fresh-water fish,
perhaps because of the rising cost of sea fish. Apart
from the luxury kinds such as trout and salmon, a
number of them are reasonably priced. Such fish
are not difficult to prepare, although some of them,
such as roach and dace, need to have the scales
scraped off with a knife. After that they can be
cleaned in much the same way as herrings. The
simplest, and I think the tastiest, way to cook them
is to roll them in seasoned flour and then fry them
until golden in a little hot butter. You can also lay
stems of fennel inside them before cooking. Served
with slices of lemon, they are lovely — but please be
sure that they are very fresh.

FISH

# Cockles in Bacon

*This was recommended as a wartime substitute for the famous oyster dish Angels on Horseback, but it is so good that it stands in its own right. It makes an excellent hors d'oeuvre, a lunch-time snack, or a buffet dish — when made in quantity, though, the problem is to keep it hot. About four little rolls per person is usually sufficient.*

A quantity of cooked cockles
Streaky bacon
Lemon juice

If you have bought cockles which are ready boiled, put them in a colander under a running cold tap for at least an hour before using them; this cleans them and removes excess salt. If raw, wash them thoroughly under the cold tap and boil them in a little unsalted water until the shells open. Throw the shells away. Put two or three cockles onto a small piece of bacon, add a squeeze of lemon juice, roll up the bacon and tie with a piece of cotton, or put several of these little rolls onto a thin skewer. Put under a hot grill for about three minutes on either side. Serve either on, or accompanied by, hot buttered toast, and garnished with parsley.

# Cockles in Tomato Sauce

Cockles
4 tomatoes
1 small tin tomato purée (or the
    equivalent homemade)
1 medium sized onion
1 clove garlic
Oil
Noodles (see page 36), spaghetti,
    or macaroni

*The same rule for cleaning the cockles given in the previous recipe still applies. No quantity of cockles is given, as they are sold in different ways in various parts of the country. But you should be able to judge the quantity easily if you buy cooked shelled cockles because there is no waste.*

Cook the pasta in the appropriate way. Chop the onion and garlic and fry gently in the oil. Chop or slice the tomatoes and add to the onion and garlic. Fry gently for 10 minutes. Stir in the tomato purée and cook for a further 10 minutes, stirring occasionally. Stir in the cockles, give them time to become thoroughly heated, and serve on top of a pile of pasta.

66

# Mussels

Mussels are usually widely available during the winter months, and are generally very cheap. Again the method of selling them varies in different parts of the country — they are sometimes sold by weight, and sometimes by the pint. You get about forty medium-sized mussels in about 4 pints which is usually enough for two, allowing for any discards. Always throw out any that are broken, open or open very easily — if too many fall into this category, complain! Scrub them thoroughly under running cold water, scrape off all barnacles, and remove the beard (the seaweed-like bits protruding from the side of the shell). Then wash in several changes of cold water until no more grit remains. An easy method of opening them is to put them into a large saucepan without any water, sprinkled with a little salt, and covered with a wet cloth. Allow them to steam very gently and they will open. Discard any that fail to open. For classic recipes such as *moules marinière*, the mussels are opened in the stock which forms the basis for the sauce.

# Mussels à la Catalane

**A quantity of mussels**
**1 medium-sized onion, minced**
**Chopped parsley stalks**
**Freshly ground black pepper**
**1 clove finely chopped garlic**
**1 oz. (30 g.) butter**
**1 oz. (30 g.) flour**
**Squeeze lemon juice**

Prepare the mussels for opening as described above, but add minced onion, garlic, parsley stalks and pepper to the pan. Steam gently. Strain the liquor which will have been produced and thicken it with butter and flour. Add a squeeze of lemon juice. Remove one shell from the mussels and arrange them on a flat dish. Serve with the sauce poured over them.

# Mussels with Pilaff

A quantity of mussels
¼ pint (150 ml.) milk
Seasoned flour
Fat or oil for frying
Savoury rice (see p. 172, but omit
   the ham)

Open the mussels as described on page 67, and when they are cold, remove from the shells, which can be discarded. Dip the mussels in the milk and coat them with seasoned flour. Fry in deep fat until golden-brown. Serve either on top of, or mixed into, savoury rice.

# Mussels à la Bordelaise

6 pints (3.6 litres) mussels
Small glass white wine
1 oz. (30 g.) butter
2 chopped shallots
1 lb. (500 g.) tomatoes
Salt and pepper
1 clove garlic
Handful chopped parsley
Handful white breadcrumbs that
   have been soaked in milk
   and strained

Open the cleaned mussels with a small glass of white wine in the pan. Melt the butter in a small saucepan and sauté the shallots. Chop the tomatoes and add them to the pan with the seasoning, the chopped garlic, the parsley and the breadcrumbs. Stir until the tomatoes are reduced to a pulp. Strain a little of the liquid from the mussels into the sauce and stir in with about a teaspoon of grated lemon peel. Remove the empty half-shell from the mussels, arrange them in a shallow fireproof dish, pour the sauce over them, and simmer for a few minutes to heat the mussels through. Serve with chunks of French bread and plenty of napkins!

# Squid or Inkfish

People are sometimes a little alarmed by the appearance of squid, but the cleaning process is not unpleasant or difficult — in fact, the anatomy is most interesting. To clean them, put them in a bowl of cold water, and gently pull the head and tentacles in one piece away from the sac-like body. The intestines which are attached to the head part can then be cut off and thrown away. There are two small ink bags each side of the head which should be removed and discarded unless the recipe calls for the ink. The purplish skin on the outside of the body and tentacles can be rubbed off with the fingers. Remove the small beak from the centre of the tentacles, and the transparent spine from the long pocket in the body. Turn the body carefully inside out and wash it under the tap to remove any sand. When ready, the flesh is very white and not at all alarming.

# Fried or Grilled Squid

*Excellent if you are able to get very small squid, not more than about 4 inches long.*

Squid
Oil
Lemon juice
Rosemary
Marjoram
Salt and black pepper

Clean the squid as described above and slice the body into rings. If the tentacles are very small leave them as they are, but, if they are long, cut them up. Put them in a shallow dish, pour over oil, plenty of lemon juice, a good sprinkling of rosemary and marjoram, and salt and pepper. Allow them to stand for at least 2 hours, turning them occasionally. Remove them from the marinade, and either dip them in seasoned flour and fry them quickly, or put them in a shallow fireproof dish and grill them. Serve very hot with sliced lemon.

# Stewed Squid

*Larger fish should be used in this recipe, and the quantities given below will provide a very tasty meal for three or four people.*

4 medium-sized squid

4 tablespoons oil (olive if possible)

2 large onions, sliced

2 cloves garlic, chopped

1 glass wine (red, white or rosé, whatever you have)

Salt and pepper

Bouquet garni (including fresh or dried fennel, if possible)

4 tomatoes

Boiled rice

Clean the fish as described above (p. 69), and cut the bodies into rounds, and slice the tentacles. Heat the oil in a heavy pan, and fry the onions and garlic gently. Put in the squid, and after a couple of minutes, add the wine and let it bubble for a minute or two. Turn the heat low. Season with salt and pepper, add the bouquet, cover the pan and cook very slowly for about one hour. You can cook them either on top of the stove or in the oven, but it must be very slowly. Shortly before the squid is cooked, chop and skin the tomatoes and reduce them to a purée with a little oil in a separate pan. Add plenty of seasoning and stir them into the squid mixture. After a couple of minutes, serve with plain boiled rice. If any squid is left over after the meal, it can be drained, dipped in seasoned flour or even in batter, fried in deep oil, and served as an excellent hors d'oeuvre.

# Meat

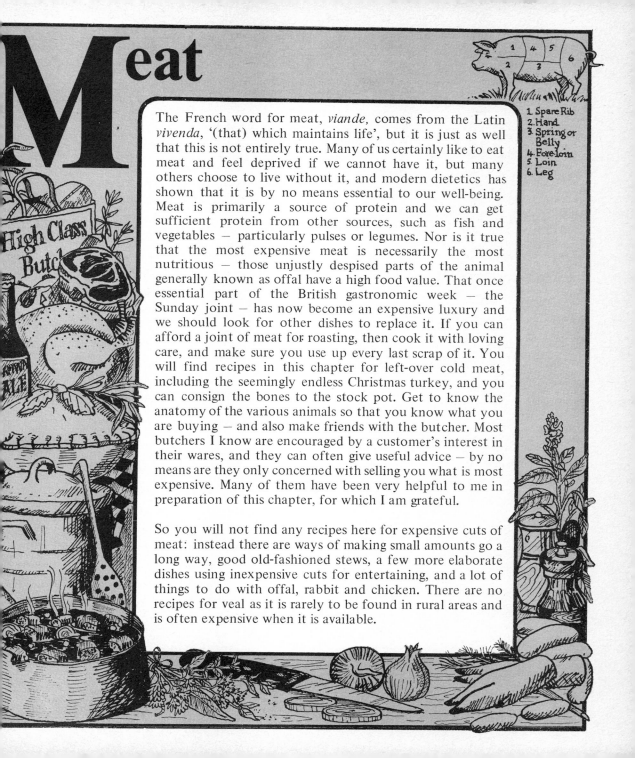

1. Spare Rib
2. Hand
3. Spring or Belly
4. Fore-loin
5. Loin
6. Leg

The French word for meat, *viande,* comes from the Latin *vivenda,* '(that) which maintains life', but it is just as well that this is not entirely true. Many of us certainly like to eat meat and feel deprived if we cannot have it, but many others choose to live without it, and modern dietetics has shown that it is by no means essential to our well-being. Meat is primarily a source of protein and we can get sufficient protein from other sources, such as fish and vegetables — particularly pulses or legumes. Nor is it true that the most expensive meat is necessarily the most nutritious — those unjustly despised parts of the animal generally known as offal have a high food value. That once essential part of the British gastronomic week — the Sunday joint — has now become an expensive luxury and we should look for other dishes to replace it. If you can afford a joint of meat for roasting, then cook it with loving care, and make sure you use up every last scrap of it. You will find recipes in this chapter for left-over cold meat, including the seemingly endless Christmas turkey, and you can consign the bones to the stock pot. Get to know the anatomy of the various animals so that you know what you are buying — and also make friends with the butcher. Most butchers I know are encouraged by a customer's interest in their wares, and they can often give useful advice — by no means are they only concerned with selling you what is most expensive. Many of them have been very helpful to me in preparation of this chapter, for which I am grateful.

So you will not find any recipes here for expensive cuts of meat: instead there are ways of making small amounts go a long way, good old-fashioned stews, a few more elaborate dishes using inexpensive cuts for entertaining, and a lot of things to do with offal, rabbit and chicken. There are no recipes for veal as it is rarely to be found in rural areas and is often expensive when it is available.

# Almundigoes

*A Scottish recipe, very good in cold weather. Serve it with whatever vegetables you have, but jacket potatoes go very well with it.*

1 lb. (500 g.) minced beef
1 large onion
1 dozen stoned raisins
¼ lb. (120 g.) stale bread
1 egg
Flour
Salt and pepper

Mince the onion and raisins and mix them well into the meat. Soak the bread in cold water, squeeze it out and mix it into the meat mixture. Season with salt and pepper, beat the egg and mix it in to bind everything together. Flour your hands and roll the mixture into small balls, roll them in flour and drop them into very hot fat to brown for a few minutes. Make a good thick gravy, drop the browned balls into it and simmer them slowly for about ¾ hour. Serve the almundigoes in the gravy.

# Jellied Moulds

*A very good way of using up leftover beef, or any other meat you may happen to have. The moulds can be served with crusty new bread and green salad, or with pickles or chutney and potato salad. The quantities given here are sufficient for about six people, so it is very economical.*

½ pint (300 ml.) good stock
½ oz. (15 g.) gelatine
1 egg
½ lb. (250 g.) cold meat
A pinch of nutmeg
Salt and pepper
1 teaspoon Worcestershire sauce
1 tablespoon chopped green herbs

Mince the meat, first removing any skin and excess fat. Hard-boil the egg and carefully slice it. Dissolve the gelatine in the usual way (or according to the instructions on the packet), and stir it into the warmed stock. Have ready individual moulds or one big one. Wet the mould or moulds and pour a layer of jelly into it. Arrange the egg in the bottom of small moulds, or around the side and on the bottom of a big mould. Leave to set. In the meantime, mix the meat with the nutmeg, the salt and pepper, Worcestershire sauce, and herbs, and stir the remaining jelly into it. Pour this mixture into the mould or moulds and leave to set. Turn out when set and garnish as you wish.

# Mock Hare

*You don't have to use port in this — a glass of red wine may be substituted. The following quantities will provide a delicious meal for four persons, and use the cheapest stewing steak you can get, provided it is not too fatty.*

1 lb. (500 g.) stewing steak
2 oz. (60 g.) bacon
1 oz. (30 g.) flour
½ pint (300 ml.) stock
A bunch of herbs
Rind and juice of half a lemon
1 dessertspoon red-currant jelly
½ glass port (or 1 glass red wine)
1 onion stuck with four cloves
1 dessertspoon chopped capers
Forcemeat balls (See page 172)
Pepper and salt

Cut the meat into neat squares and toss them in seasoned flour. Dice the bacon, and fry it for a few minutes in a large heavy pan. Add the meat and stir it until browned. Pour in the stock, and the wine (but not port, if you are using it), add the herbs, the grated lemon rind and the onion. Cover the pan and simmer very gently for about 1½ hours, or until the meat is tender. About five minutes before serving, stir in the port, lemon juice and the red-currant jelly. Put the meat in a hot serving dish, strain over the gravy, sprinkle with the capers and garnish with forcemeat balls.

# Dolmas

*Ideally these should be cooked in vine leaves, but these are not very easy to find outside large towns. I once saw this recipe translated as 'stuffed vain lives', but here we will make do with cabbage leaves.*

½ lb. (250 g.) minced beef
1 clove garlic
Pinch fresh thyme (less, if dried)
Salt and black pepper
2 tablespoons rice
Cabbage leaves

Mix the meat with the rice, garlic, thyme and seasonings. Blanch the cabbage leaves in boiling water, and cut out the centre rib. If the leaves are very big, cut them in half. Put 1 teaspoon of the meat mixture on to each leaf, and fold the leaves to make neat little parcels. Pack them closely into a pan, and barely cover them with water, or thin tomato sauce. Cover and simmer for about 1½ hours. These are very good cooked in water and then served with Avgolemono (egg and lemon) sauce (see page 177).

# Sea Pie

*A delicious and filling dish, needing no accompaniments. You can use whatever vegetables you happen to have, but do remember that the haricot beans, or split peas have to be soaked overnight.*

4 oz. (120 g.) haricot beans or
    yellow split peas
½ – 1 lb. (250 – 500 g.) stewing
    steak (or neck of lamb)
1 onion or leek
2 carrots
1 turnip
1 stalk of celery
1 oz. (30 g.) flour
Salt and freshly ground black
    pepper
1 pint (600 ml.) stock (or water)

For the crust:
8 oz. (250 g.) flour
2 oz. (60 g.) shredded suet
½ teaspoonful baking powder
Cold water
Salt and pepper

Cut the meat into small squares, dice or slice the fresh vegetables and mix with the meat. Mix the 1 oz. (30 g.) flour with the salt and pepper. Fill a straight-sided casserole, or a saucepan with layers of the meat and vegetables, and the beans or peas. Sprinkle the seasoned flour over the top and pour in the stock so that the mixture is barely covered. Make the crust:
Mix the flour, suet, seasoning and baking powder with enough water to make a light dough. Roll it out so that it is about 1 in. smaller than the casserole or saucepan. Bring the meat and vegetables to the boil, place the crust on top, and cover with a close-fitting lid. Simmer for about 2 – 2½ hours. Serve with the crust cut into triangular pieces, like cake.

# Ravioli

*Another do-it-yourself pasta. A little bit fiddly, but so much cheaper than buying ravioli ready-made, and very impressive!*

Mix the flour with a quarter of a teaspoon of salt. Rub in the fat. Add the beaten egg, with sufficient liquid to make a stiff dough, then knead until it is completely smooth. Divide the dough into two, and roll each piece thinly into a large square. Bind the minced meat with a little gravy or sauce and season it well. Place teaspoonfuls at intervals on one of the pieces of paste — space them out evenly about ½ in. apart. Moisten the paste between the little heaps with a pastry brush and cold water. Brush the other piece of paste with cold water and place it wet side down on top of the meat. Press it well down round the little heaps of meat, so that each is thoroughly enclosed. With a sharp knife, cut between the heaps so that you have lots of little cushions. Press all edges well together, expelling any air bubbles. Spread the ravioli on a rack and leave in a cool dry place for several hours (overnight) before cooking it. To cook it, boil for 15—20 minutes in fast-boiling salted water, and serve with a tomato sauce, and sprinkled with grated cheese.

4 oz. (120 g.) flour

Salt and pepper

½ oz. (15 g.) butter

Half an egg

Milk and water, or water to mix

A little gravy or sauce

2 oz. (60 g.) minced cooked meat

Grated cheese (Parmesan, if
    possible)

Sauce to serve

# Carbonnade of Beef

*A tasty Belgian recipe. It is very filling, and goes well with plain boiled, or jacket potatoes, and followed by a green salad.*

Melt the dripping and fry the onions until they are brown. Remove from the pan, and keep hot. Cut the steak into squares and brown all over in the pan, remove and keep with the onions. Pour the beer into the pan and cook it without a lid until the liquid is reduced to about one-third of its original quantity. Stir in the sauce and the gravy and boil for about three minutes. Add the onions and the meat together with the seasoning and the *bouquet.* Cover and simmer gently for about 2 hours, until the meat is very tender. Remove the *bouquet* before serving.

2 oz. (60 g.) dripping

4 sliced onions

½ lb. (250 g.) stewing steak

1 pint (600 ml.) bottle of brown ale

¼ pint (150 ml.) tomato sauce

½ pint (300 ml.) brown gravy

Salt and pepper

A *bouquet garni* (parsley, marjoram
    thyme and a bay leaf)

# Chinese Beef and Cabbage

*Ideal for stretching a small amount of beef with vegetables. It is important that the meat and the cabbage should be shredded into very small pieces, so that it does not take long to cook. The quantities given here will serve four people.*

½ lb. (250 g.) lean beef
1 small white cabbage
1 medium-sized onion
2 cloves garlic
Small piece stem ginger
¼ lb. (125 g.) mushrooms
2 tablespoons soy sauce
A dash of vinegar
Cornflour
Oil
Rice for four

Cook the rice according to your usual method. Cut the meat into very small pieces — about the size of a matchstick is best. Shred the cabbage as finely as you can — you can include the stalk. Chop the onion, garlic and ginger finely. Heat a little oil in a frying pan and gently fry the garlic and ginger for a few minutes. Add the onion and the beef and keep stirring while it browns lightly. Add the cabbage and stir for about three minutes. Stir the cornflour into a spoonful of hot water, and when it is smooth, add it to the mixture in the frying-pan. Stir in the soy sauce and continue stirring so that it is well mixed. Add the mushrooms and leave this to simmer while you drain the rice. If the meat seems too dry, moisten it with a little hot water, more soy sauce and a dash of vinegar. Serve piled on top of the rice, in small bowls.

# Pork Chops Baked with Potatoes

*A rustic French dish, with a delicious flavour — allow one chop per person, and serve whatever vegetables you have. Use spare rib chops — they are usually the cheapest.*

Peel the potatoes and slice them thinly and evenly. Slice the onion. Arrange half the potatoes and half the onions in the bottom of an earthenware casserole. Insert a juniper berry and a small piece of garlic into each chop near the bone. Brown the chops on each side in a little oil (or pork dripping).

4 pork chops
1½ lb. (750 g.) potatoes
A small glass white wine or cider
2 cloves garlic
A few juniper berries, if possible
Parsley
4 oz. (120 g.) bacon
1 onion

Put the chops on top of the potatoes and cover them with the remaining onion and potatoes. Cover with the bacon, cut in slices. Pour over the wine or cider. Put two or three layers of greaseproof paper over the pot and then the lid. Cook in a very slow oven (Gas mark 1, Electric 275°F., 140°C.) for about three hours. Before serving, pour off some of the abundant fat which will have come from the meat, and garnish with some nice sprigs of fresh parsley.

# Instant Djuveč

*A quick, and economical, version of the classic Yugoslavian dish. The original uses pork, lamb, and beef and is cooked for a long time in the oven, and very good it is. This version takes a short time to cook and uses only belly pork, but it is quite delicious, and includes a variety of fresh vegetables.*

1 lb. (500 g.) belly pork
1 large onion
1 clove garlic
1 stick of celery
2 carrots
1 green pepper
2 large tomatoes
1 cooking apple
Rice
Oil for frying

Boil the rice according to your usual method. In the meantime, remove the rind from the pork and cut it into small pieces. Heat the oil in a thick pan, and gently fry the sliced onions and garlic. When the onion begins to look transparent, add the sliced tomatoes, the carrots cut into rings, the celery cut into small pieces, the pepper, seeded, and cut into rings and the sliced apple. Allow the mixture to cook gently for about twenty minutes — it should be stewed, not fried. At the same time, fry the pork gently in its own fat. When everything is cooked, drain the rice and the pork and mix the two together. Last of all, stir in the vegetables, with their juice, making sure that all ingredients are mixed well together. Pile it into a hot serving dish, add a good sprinkling of parsley, and serve with good crusty French bread.

# Scalloped Pork with Cabbage

*In my experience, pork is rarely left over, but should you find yourself with some, here is what to do with it.*

1 lb. (500 g.) lean cooked pork
1 lb. (500 g.) cabbage
1 oz. (30 g.) butter
1 oz. (30 g.) flour
1 pint (600 ml.) stock or milk
Salt and pepper
Pinch of mace or nutmeg
½ pint (300 ml.) fresh white
  breadcrumbs
½ oz. (15 g.) butter

Wash and slice the cabbage in ¼ in. strips. Trim and slice the meat. Melt the ½ oz. (15 g.) butter in a frying pan, add the crumbs, stir and heat gently until well coated. Cook the cabbage in about 1in. boiling salted water with the lid on for no longer than 8 minutes, when the cabbage should be just tender. Drain it. Keep the liquid for making the sauce. Melt the 1 oz. (30 g.) butter in a small pan, add the flour and cook, stirring, for a couple of minutes. Add the cabbage liquid, together with enough milk to make up 1 pint (600 ml.), and stir until it boils. Boil for about 3 minutes, then add the mace or nutmeg, and salt and pepper to taste. Arrange the pork and the cabbage in alternate layers in a fireproof dish and pour over the sauce. Cover the top with the breadcrumbs, and bake in a moderately hot oven (Gas mark 6, Electric 400°F., 200°C.) until the top is nicely browned (about 20 minutes).

# Pork and Onion Dumpling

*A good meal for cold weather; not very elegant, perhaps, but very satisfying. If you cook root vegetables in the same pan as the dumpling, you have a complete meal.*

Roll the pastry into a circle. Peel and slice the onions thinly. Cut the pork into medium sized squares, removing excess fat. Put half the onions in the centre of the pastry and sprinkle with salt and pepper and half the sage. Put the pork on top,

8 oz. (250 g.) suet pastry
(see page 169)

3 onions

1 lb. (500 g.) spare-rib or neck
of pork

½ teaspoon powdered sage

Salt and black pepper

and then more salt and pepper, the remaining sage and the rest of the onion. Dampen the edges of the pastry, and gather them up pinching them securely together. Press gently with floured hands to make a nice, smooth ball. Flour a pudding cloth and place the dumpling in the centre. Gather the cloth up, and tie it loosely, but securely with string. Do be careful not to have the cloth tight, as the dumpling will swell while cooking. Boil for 2 — 2½ hours.

# Garbure

*This is really a pork stew. It is very nourishing, and you can add any vegetables you have to this basic recipe, or serve them separately. You can use the equivalent weight of boiling bacon if you like, but I prefer it with pork. One of those packaged pork boiling sausages can be used instead of garlic sausage.*

1 lb. (500 g.) belly pork

¼ lb. (120 g.) garlic sausage

1 cabbage

½ lb. (250 g.) potatoes

½ lb. (250 g.) haricot beans

2 or 3 cloves garlic

Salt and pepper

Thyme and marjoram

Water or stock (if available)

Soak the haricot beans overnight. Drain them and cover them with clean cold water. Bring slowly to the boil and simmer them with a lid on for about 1 hour. Peel the potatoes and cut them into fairly large pieces and add them to the beans, together with the meat in one piece, the herbs, garlic, salt and pepper. If you decide to use any other root vegetables they should also be added at this stage. Any stock should also be added now, and the whole simmered for another hour. Shred the cabbage finely, stir it into the pan and cook for a further ½ hour. Remove the meat and slice it, and serve with the vegetables in a separate dish. Any left-overs can be made into soup by the addition of stock or water.

# Pork Sausage Galantine

1 lb. (500 g.) pork sausage meat

2 oz. (60 g.) lean bacon

1 egg

4 level tablespoons dried breadcrumbs

2 teaspoons chopped parsley

Pinch dried herbs

1 tablespoon chutney

1 teaspoon Worcester sauce

1 level teaspoon dry mustard

Stock to moisten

*A useful dish for any time you want to serve cold sliced meat. It can be accompanied by any salad, or pickles and chutneys.*

Remove the rind from the bacon and chop it finely. Beat the egg. Mix all the ingredients together in a basin, adding enough stock to make a fairly soft mixture, and when everything is thoroughly mixed, pack it into a greased 1 lb. (500 g.) loaf tin. Make a lid of foil and steam for 1½ hours. Leave to cool in the tin, and store in a cold place.

# Lentils with Bacon

*A dish which never fails to please — it is very nourishing, and filling and I find that people can rarely eat much afterwards, so you need only provide cheese and fruit. The quantities given here are ample for six.*

1½ lb. (750 g.) boiling bacon

Some dripping

A dozen or more small onions

Freshly ground black pepper

1 lb. (500 g.) brown lentils

1 carrot, 1 stick celery

A bunch fresh herbs

2 cloves garlic, crushed

1 oz. (30 g.) butter

Chopped parsley

Hard-boiled eggs (optional)

Put the bacon into a large saucepan and cover it with cold water. Bring it to the boil, strain it, rinse it in cold water and dry it. Melt a little dripping in a deep casserole and put in the bacon and the onions, sprinkled with black pepper. When the onions start to brown, add the lentils, the carrot, cut in two, the celery, the herbs and the garlic. Cover with cold water, cover with a lid and cook very slowly for about 2 hours. Take out the bacon, and discard the herbs, carrot and celery. Strain the lentils and stir in the butter. Arrange them on a hot serving dish, with the sliced bacon on top. Garnish with chopped parsley and halved hard-boiled eggs, if you wish.

# Bacon Hotpot

*An English version of the American pork and beans, using butter beans instead of haricots. It needs no accompaniments, and need only be followed by salad, and/or fresh fruit.*

6 oz. (180 g.) butter beans
1½ lb. (750 g.) boiling bacon
1 pint (600 ml.) good stock
1 large onion
2 stalks celery
½ level teaspoon dry mustard
¼ level teaspoon black pepper
1 or 2 tablespoons black treacle

Soak the beans and the bacon separately overnight in plenty of cold water. Drain and cut the bacon into four pieces, putting it, with the beans into a casserole. Peel and slice the onion and wash and chop the celery, and add them to the casserole. Mix the mustard with some of the stock, mix in the pepper and the treacle, and pour over the meat and vegetables. Add enough stock to cover. Put the lid on and cook at Gas mark 1, Electric 275°F., 140°C., for 2 hours. Remove the lid from the casserole and lift the pieces of meat to the top. Cook for another hour to brown the meat, and serve from the casserole.

# Braised Spare Ribs of Pork

*This recipe is adapted from one in a Ministry of Food leaflet called Making the Most of Meat. It needs only plain boiled potatoes or rice as an accompaniment.*

2 lbs. (1 kg.) spare ribs
1 oz. (30 g.) fat or dripping
2 medium onions, sliced
4 oz. (120 g.) tomatoes
½ teaspoon ground mace
½ teaspoon ground nutmeg
1 medium apple, sliced
8 oz. (250 g.) mixed carrot and
   turnip, diced
1 teaspoon salt
Pinch of black pepper
1 pint (600 ml.) stock or water

Trim off any surplus fat from the meat. Heat the fat or dripping in a pan and brown the meat all over. Lift out the meat and fry the onions, tomatoes, apple, carrot and turnip lightly in the same fat. Then season the vegetables and add the mace and nutmeg. Mix thoroughly and add the stock or water (which should not completely cover the vegetables). Place the meat on top – it should be above the level of the liquid. Cover the pan and cook very slowly until the meat is tender (about 1 hour). When cooked, arrange the ribs in the centre of a serving dish with the vegetables around the edge, and pour the gravy over the meat.

# Suliman's Pilaff

*A useful dish for serving a lot of people — children like it very much, and it is very economical. I serve it with a bowl of yoghurt and follow it with salad, and a light sweet — or just fruit and cheese.*

2 cupfuls rice

4 tablespoons dripping or oil

½ lb. (250 g.) cooked lamb or
    mutton cut into small pieces

1 large onion, sliced and fried

1 cupful stoned raisins

½ cupful currants

2 cloves garlic, chopped and fried

4 tomatoes, chopped

½ cupful pine nuts (or if you
    can't get them, roasted
    almonds)

Salt

Freshly ground black pepper

Put the dripping into a thick saucepan and when it has warmed put in the rice. Stir it for a few minutes until it begins to look transparent and then pour over 4 pints (2.5 litres) boiling water, and cook very fast for about 12 minutes. Be careful not to overcook the rice. In the meantime, sauté all the other ingredients in plenty of dripping with plenty of salt and pepper. Strain the rice, wash out the pan, and return the rice to it. Stir in the meat and onion mixture and continue stirring over a low flame for a few minutes before serving.

# Roast Neck of Lamb

*Persuade your butcher not to cut all the Best End into cutlets, but to let you have a whole piece, but ask him to chine it, and remove the skin. One neck of lamb will feed four to six people.*

A neck of lamb

Enough buttered greaseproof
    paper to wrap the meat

Finely chopped parsley

Maitre d'hotel sauce (see page 176)

Steamed cucumber (see page 133)

Wrap the meat in the paper and roast it in a hot oven (Gas mark 7, Electric 425°F., 220°C.) allowing 15 minutes to the pound (30 mins. per kilogram). When it is cooked, remove the paper and put it on a hot serving dish. Pour maitre d'hotel sauce around it, and sprinkle the parsley on top. Garnish it with steamed cucumbers.

# Epigrams of Lamb

*An unusual way of cooking breasts of lamb. The sherry can, of course, be omitted from the sauce but, since the rest of the ingredients are very cheap, I think it is worth including. It is a good idea to cook the meat the day before you plan to eat it.*

Put the meat into a large saucepan with the sliced carrot, the peeled onion, the *bouquet,* peppercorns and half a teaspoon of salt. Barely cover with water and simmer until the meat is tender — be careful not to cook it to pieces — just tender enough to draw out the bones easily. When cooked, lift the meat onto a flat dish, remove the bones, and sprinkle it with the chopped mushrooms, shallot and parsley. Season it with salt to taste, and with cayenne. Put another dish on top of the meat with a weight on top so that the meat is pressed flat. Leave overnight. Strain the stock in which the meat has cooked, and when it is quite cold, remove the fat from the top. Use ½ pint (300 ml.) of this stock as the base for the sauce. Blend the flour with a little of the stock, heat the remainder in a saucepan, and thicken it with the flour mixture. Add the red currant jelly, the mushroom ketchup, and the sherry.

When the meat is cold and set, cut it into rings with a sharp pastry cutter (about the size of a tumbler). Dip the rounds into beaten egg, and then into white breadcrumbs. Fry these rounds golden-brown in smoking hot fat. Drain them well and arrange them on a hot dish with mashed potato in a border all round, and serve with the hot sauce strained over.

1 ½ lb. (750 g.) breast of lamb
1 small carrot
A *bouquet garni* (bay leaf, thyme
     and parsley) and 1 tablespoon
     chopped parsley
1 onion
1 shallot
2 large mushrooms
1 egg
Breadcrumbs
4 black peppercorns
Salt and cayenne

For the sauce:
1 oz. (30 g.) flour
1 teaspoon red currant jelly
1 teaspoon mushroom ketchup
1 dessertspoon sherry

# German Cutlets

*A good way of making your meat go further —
these quantities will feed six people. It is a little
bit fiddly to do, but the end result looks very
impressive and appetising.*

Mince the lamb and the ham very finely. Put the
stock into a saucepan, with the herbs (bayleaf,
thyme, and parsley), the meat extract, the onion,
cloves and peppercorns. Boil until the liquid is
reduced to about ½ pint (300 ml.), strain it and
dissolve the gelatine in it. Melt the butter in a
saucepan and stir in the flour. Add the stock a
little at a time, stirring all the time. Now mix in
the minced meat, and the parsley, cayenne and
salt to taste. Make sure that everything is thoroughly
mixed together and then turn out on to a flat dish
to cool. When the mixture has set, take pieces
about the size of an egg, roll them in flour and form
them into the shape of a cutlet or chop. Egg and
breadcrumb each cutlet twice so that it is thickly
coated. Deep fry them until they are a nice golden-
brown. If you are cooking for a special occasion, it
is a good idea to put a little paper frill on the thin
end of each cutlet, but that is entirely up to you. A
good way of serving them is to arrange a border of
of mashed potatoes on the serving dish, lay the
cutlets on top, and fill the middle with green French
beans — then pour tomato sauce (see page 178) all
over everything.

1 lb. (500 g.) cold lamb

2 oz. (60 g.) lean ham

1 teaspoon parsley

1 teaspoon meat extract

⅛ oz. (5 g.) gelatine

2 oz. (60 g.) butter

1 oz. (30 g.) flour

¾ pint (450 ml.) diluted stock

1 small onion

2 cloves and 4 peppercorns

A bunch of herbs

Salt, pepper, and cayenne

1 egg

Breadcrumbs

Oil for frying

Mashed potatoes

# Lamb Shashlik

*For this dish, the meat should be marinaded overnight.
You will need fairly fine skewers about 10 in. long.
The quantities given will serve six people, and you
can serve the shashliks with plain boiled rice, or with
a risotto, green salad, or sliced green peppers.*

Cut the meat into 1½ in. cubes, trimming off most of the fat. Peel and slice the onions. Put the meat into a bowl with the onion, salt and pepper, lemon juice and cider. Leave overnight in a cold place. Next day, wash the tomatoes and the mushrooms and thread the meat on skewers, alternating with a small whole tomato (or half a large one), and a mushroom. Grill for 15 minutes turning the shashliks once. You can serve on the skewers or not, as you wish. The easiest way to remove the skewers is to place the shashlik on a plate, put another plate upside down on top, with the end of the skewer protruding, then pull the skewers out while holding the two plates together.

2 lb. (1 kg.) boned lamb

2 small onions

1 level teaspoon salt

½ teaspoon black pepper

Juice of 1 lemon

2 tablespoons cider (or white wine)

8 small tomatoes

8 mushrooms

# Spring Stew

*A wonderful stew to make when spring vegetables are plentiful. Full of nourishment and as useful for a dinner party as it is for a family meal.*

Bone the lamb and cut it into squares. Melt the dripping in a large heavy pan and put in the onions and meat. When they are golden, remove them from the pan and keep them hot. Stir the flour into the fat until you have a light brown roux, add the stock and stir until the sauce has amalgamated. Put back the onions and meat and add the salt, pepper, the rosemary, the garlic and the bayleaf. Cover and simmer for about one hour when the meat should be nearly cooked. Add the potatoes (which need only have been scrubbed), the carrots (whole), and the turnips (which need not be cut unless they are fairly big). Cook slowly for about 35 minutes, while you are shelling the peas. Add the peas and as soon as they are cooked the stew is ready. It is a very substantial meal, and need only be followed by a very light dessert.

3 lb. (1.5 kg.) breast of lamb

1 lb. (500 g.) small new potatoes

A small bunch baby carrots

A few baby turnips

1½ lb. (750 g.) green peas

3 small onions (sliced)

3 tablespoons good dripping

2 tablespoons flour

1 pint (600 ml.) brown stock

Salt and black pepper

A sprig rosemary

1 clove garlic (crushed)

1 bayleaf

# Lamb Patties

*A good way of using up cold cooked meat — it doesn't have to be lamb, of course, but whatever you happen to have.*

6 oz. (180 g.) shortcrust pastry
8 oz. (250 g.) cooked minced lamb
1 medium-sized onion, chopped
1 level teaspoon capers
½ teaspoon freshly made mustard
Salt and pepper
A little gravy or stock
1 tomato (optional)

Roll out the pastry to line six patty tins, reserving some for lids. Mix together the meat, onion, capers, mustard, and salt and pepper to taste. Moisten with a little gravy or stock (or tomato sauce, if you happen to have any). Fill each of the lined patty tins, and, if you wish, put a slice of tomato on top of the meat before putting the lid on. Cover with the pastry lids, making sure that the edges are well sealed. Make a small hole in the top of each patty, and bake in a fairly hot oven (Gas mark 6, Electric 400°F., 200°C.) for about 20 minutes, or until the pastry is nicely browned.

# Irish Stew

*A good old-fashioned standby — but how delicious it can be. The quantities given will serve about six people, as long as they are not too greedy. There are sufficient potatoes in the stew, so you need only serve green vegetables and/or carrots as an accompaniment.*

2 lb. (1 kg.) lamb or mutton —
    use breast or neck of lamb
1 level tablespoon salt
½ level teaspoon black pepper
2 lb. (1 kg.) potatoes
2 large onions
1 tablespoon chopped parsley

Trim away excess fat from the meat and cut it up into convenient pieces for serving. Peel and chop the onions. Peel the potatoes and cut them into thickish slices. Put a layer of meat into the bottom of a casserole, season with pepper and salt. Add a layer of potatoes and then a layer of onions. Repeat these layers until you have used everything up. Add sufficient water to come three-quarters of the way up the meat and vegetables. Cover and simmer for about 1½ hours, or until the meat is tender. This can be done on top of the cooker or in the oven. Turn out into a hot dish and serve with a thick sprinkling of parsley.

# Hearts

All hearts need slow cooking to make them tender — ox heart takes longest as it is the largest. One ox heart will serve five or six people, a calf's or sheep's one or two, and a lamb's one person.

# Baked Ox Heart or Calf's Heart

*This dish also goes under the delightful name of 'Love in Disguise'. I have mostly used ox heart for it, but bear in mind that if you should use calf's heart, it will only take half as long to cook. The quantities given are for an ox heart — you should halve them for a calf's heart.*

Cut all the gristle and tubes out of the heart, and cut the internal membranes so that there is one cavity for the stuffing. Soak overnight in cold water. Drain and dry. Make the stuffing and stuff the heart. Sew up the opening with a needle and coarse thread (white thread is best, so that it shows up). Wrap the rashers around the heart, wrap it in foil and bake in a moderate oven (Gas mark 4, Electric 350°F., 180°C.), for about 2½ hours. Meanwhile, break the vermicelli into small pieces and boil it in plenty of salted water. Drain and leave to cool, and mix with the breadcrumbs. When the heart is cooked, remove the foil, brush it with the beaten egg yolks and roll it in the vermicelli mixture so that it is well coated. Put back in the baking tin, and bake until brown, basting from time to time. Serve with jacket potatoes and baked tomatoes.

1 ox heart

Sage and onion stuffing
   (see page 172)

6 rashers fat bacon

2 oz. (60 g.) vermicelli

2 oz. (60 g.) fresh breadcrumbs

2 egg yolks

# Lambs' Hearts, Stuffed and Baked

Allow one or two hearts per person, cut out the coarse tubes and excess fat. Wash them thoroughly in warm salted water, and stuff the cavity with sage and onion stuffing (see page 172). Wrap a rasher of fat bacon around each heart, wrap them in foil and bake in a moderate oven (Gas mark 4, Electric 350°F., 180°C.) for about 1 – 1½ hours.

# Braised Stuffed Hearts

4 sheep's hearts or 8 lamb's
    hearts

8 oz. (250 g.) breadcrumbs

2 oz. (60 g.) suet

3 tablespoons chopped parsley

Salt and freshly ground pepper

1 egg

2 oz. (60 g.) dripping

2 large onions, 2 carrots,
    2 turnips

1 oz. (30 g.) flour

1 pint (600 ml.) stock

1 lb. (500 g.) potatoes

1 cauliflower

½ lb. (250 g.) brussel sprouts

Wash and clean the hearts, removing any coarse tubes, and cut through the inner membranes so that there is a cavity left for stuffing. Mix together the breadcrumbs, the suet and the parsley, season well and bind with the beaten egg. Stuff the hearts with this mixture and stitch the tops with coarse white thread. Melt the dripping in a pan, cut up the onions, carrots and the turnips and sauté them in the dripping. Put them in a casserole. Fry the hearts in the dripping until they are well-browned and put them on top of the vegetables in the casserole. Make a gravy with the fat left in the pan, the flour and the stock, season it well and pour it over the hearts. Cover the casserole and cook either on top of the cooker or in a moderate oven (Gas mark 4, Electric 350°F., 180°C.) for about 1½ hours. In the meantime, boil and mash the potatoes so that they are very creamy. Cook the cauliflower and the sprouts. When the hearts are cooked, put the vegetables from the casserole in the bottom of a hot serving dish, pipe the potato over them in rows, and put the hearts between each row of potato. Garnish with the cauliflower and sprouts and serve with the strained gravy. A very substantial dish needing no further accompaniments.

# Tripe

Tripe comes from the lining of the ox stomach, and is a light, easily digested meat — it was often recommended for invalids. The varieties of tripe have delightful names, such as honeycomb and monk's head, but the differences are in appearance rather than taste. It is almost always sold dressed and partly cooked, so that it is a whitish colour. It is very economical, as there is no waste. 4 to 6 oz. (120 g. to 180 g.) per person is usually ample. Put it into a saucepan covered with cold water, bring it to the boil, pour off the water and cover again with fresh cold water. Simmer slowly for about 2 hours until it is tender, and it is then ready to be further cooked in a variety of ways.

## Tripe Wiggle

1 lb. (500 g.) tripe
½ pint (300 ml.) white sauce
1 cupful peeled shrimps or
    prawns (tinned ones will do)
Salt and black pepper
A pinch mace
A squeeze lemon juice
Parsley and lemon slices to garnish

Prepare the tripe as described above and keep the liquor in which it has been cooked. Cut the tripe into small squares. Make a good white sauce, using 1 oz. (30 g.) butter, 1 oz. (30 g.) flour and ½ pint (300 ml.) milk and tripe liquor mixed. When the sauce is cooked stir in the tripe and the shrimps and season to taste with salt and pepper, mace and lemon juice. Cook gently for a few minutes and serve in a shallow dish garnished with plenty of parsley and slices of lemon.

## Tripe and Bacon Rolls

1 lb. (500 g.) tripe
6 rashers bacon
1 large onion, chopped
Parsley
½ pint (300 ml.) stock
½ oz. (15 g.) flour

Cut the tripe into strips about 3 in. wide, lay a rasher of bacon on each, sprinkle with chopped onion and parsley, roll up and tie firmly with string. Put into a saucepan, cover with stock and simmer for one hour. Remove the rolls from the stock, take off the string and keep them hot. Thicken the liquor with flour and serve the rolls piled in the centre of a border of mashed potato, with the sauce poured over, and sprinkled with chopped parsley.

# Malayan Curried Tripe

1 lb. (500 g.) tripe

1 tablespoon vinegar

1 tablespoon coriander seeds

2 teaspoons ground turmeric

A pinch ground cumin

1 teaspoon ground mustard seed

1 teaspoon ground black pepper

1 oz. (30 g.) fat

1 onion

1 clove garlic

2 oz. (60 g.) desiccated coconut
   soaked in boiling water for
   15 minutes

2 teaspoons mango chutney

A little stock

Salt

*An unusual way of cooking tripe — and a very good way of disguising it if you are serving people who claim not to like it!*

Cook the tripe in the usual way (see page 89), and cut it into small, neat pieces. Make a paste with the vinegar, coriander seeds, turmeric, cumin, mustard and pepper. Melt the fat in a frying pan, and fry the chopped onion and garlic. Add the paste and stir thoroughly, then cook gently for about 4 minutes. Add the strained coconut milk, the chutney, the tripe and enough stock to make a good thick gravy. Season with salt, make sure it has thoroughly heated through, and serve with plain, boiled rice.

# Tripe and Mushrooms

Cook the tripe in the usual way, and cut it into narrow strips about 2 in. long. Put the strips to soak in the vinegar and oil for about ½ hour. In the meantime wash the mushrooms and cut them into thin slices. Heat 1½ oz. (45 g.) butter in a saucepan and brown the chopped shallot in it. Add the mushrooms, cook them for about 3 minutes and lift them out. Leave them to drain in a warm place. Add the flour to the fat left in the pan, and stir it until it is smooth, add the tomatoes and cook until the sauce thickens. Season to taste and, if you wish, strain before using. (I find the dish is more substantial if

1 lb. (500 g.) tripe

2 tablespoons vinegar

2 tablespoons oil

½ lb. (250 g.) mushrooms

2 oz. (60 g.) butter

1 shallot

1 oz. (30 g.) flour

1 medium tin tomatoes

Salt and black pepper

1 cupful breadcrumbs

you don't strain the sauce — it seems a waste to strain off the shallot and the tomato skins). Grease a fairly shallow fireproof dish, and put a layer of the tripe in the bottom. Cover lightly with tomato sauce, then the mushrooms, another thin layer of sauce, and sprinkle with half the breadcrumbs. Over this lay the rest of the tripe, the remainder of the sauce and cover with breadcrumbs. Dot with the remaining butter and bake uncovered for ½ hour in a hot oven (Gas mark 8, Electric 450°F., 230°C.). It should be served when nicely browned.

# Liver à la Crème

*Although the recipe states calf's liver, obviously you can use whichever kind of liver you like, depending on your purse and preference. Calf's liver is generally considered to be the most delicate, but I find that lamb's or pig's are generally more popular.*

1 lb. (500 g.) calf's liver

1 onion

2 carrots

1 stalk celery

1 oz. (30 g.) oil for frying

1 tablespoon chopped parsley

A pinch thyme

1 bayleaf

Salt

1 small glass vinegar

1 cup sour cream

2 tablespoons breadcrumbs

Stock (if necessary)

Wash the liver and cut out any tubes; dry it. Cut it into slices about ¼ in. thick. Slice the onion, carrots and celery. Heat the oil in a frying pan and gently fry the onion, carrot and celery, with the parsley, thyme and bayleaf. Add the liver and salt, and stew gently for about 10 minutes. Add the vinegar, sour cream, and the breadcrumbs, and continue to cook slowly until the liver is tender. Add stock if it becomes too dry. Serve with vegetables of your own choice.

# Paupiettes of Lamb's Liver

½ lb. (250 g.) lamb's liver
½ lb. (250 g.) rashers of bacon
4 tomatoes, or a small cup
  tomato sauce (freshly
  made — see page 178)
1 glass red wine
¼ pint (150 ml.) meat stock
1 oz. (30 g.) butter
½ oz. (15 g.) flour
Fresh thyme or marjoram
Lemon juice
Salt and freshly ground black
  pepper
Small skewers

*It is best to buy the liver in one piece for this recipe so that you can slice it yourself. Serve the paupiettes with plain boiled rice, or with sautéed potatoes, and followed by salad.*

Wash the liver and cut it into very thin slices, a little smaller than the rashers of bacon. On each rasher lay a slice of liver, season it with a little salt, pepper and lemon juice. Sprinkle with thyme or marjoram. Roll up, with the bacon on the outside and secure the little rolls with small skewers (or string, if you have no skewers). Heat the butter in a frying-pan and sauté the *paupiettes.* Sprinkle in the flour and stir in the red wine. Let it bubble for a few minutes, then add either the tomatoes, which you have skinned and chopped small, or the sauce. Stir gently and add add the stock. Cover the pan and cook very gently for about 10 minutes. Remove the skewers or the string, and serve very hot.

# Mexican Liver

*This is a good way of cooking ox liver, and you can use a small tin of red peppers if fresh ones are too expensive.*

Melt the dripping in a frying pan, and fry the sliced liver lightly. Remove the liver and put it into a casserole. Slice the onions and the tomato, and, if you are using fresh peppers, take the seeds out and slice them. Fry these in the pan until they are quite soft, but do not add tinned peppers at this stage — they are very soft already. Add onions, tomato, and peppers to the liver in the casserole.

¾ lb. (360 g.) liver

2 oz. (60 g.) dripping

2 onions

4 red peppers

1 large tomato (skinned)

1 oz. (30 g.) flour

½ pint (300 ml.) stock

Salt and pepper

2 oz. (60 g.) rice

Make a sauce with the fat left in the pan, by stirring in the flour and gradually adding the stock. Season well with salt and pepper and pour the stock into the casserole. Cover the casserole and simmer gently for about ¾ hour. Meanwhile, boil the rice in the usual way. It is a good idea to reserve a few rings of pepper, to cook them gently at this stage, so that they can be used as a garnish. Arrange the cooked, drained rice on a hot serving dish so that it forms a ring, and pile the liver mixture in the middle. Garnish with the rings of pepper, and serve very hot. This dish needs no accompaniments.

# Mock Goose

*A substantial dish, requiring only seasonal vegetables to accompany it. I am not convinced that it tastes anything like goose, but it is very good. Another name for it is Poor Man's Goose.*

1 lb. (500 g.) ox liver

2 large onions

4 oz. (120 g.) fatty bacon

1 tablespoon flour, seasoned
    with salt and black pepper

1 dessertspoon chopped fresh sage

2 lb. (1 kg.) potatoes

Dripping

Wash the liver and cut out any tubes, then cut it into slices about ¼ in. thick. Slice the onion and cut the bacon into 1 in. squares. Toss the liver in the seasoned flour and fill a pie dish with alternate layers of liver, bacon, onions and sage. Peel and slice the potatoes fairly thinly, and cover the layers of liver with a thick layer of potatoes. Add enough water to come just below the potatoes, and dot with small pieces of dripping. Cover the dish with greased paper and bake in a moderate oven (Gas mark 4, Electric 350°F., 180°C.) for about two hours. Twenty minutes before the cooking time is up, remove the paper so that the potatoes will brown.

# Ox Kidney with Baked Haricot Beans

*A good cheap dish, and very nourishing. It has to be cooked for a long time, but at a very low temperature, so does not use a lot of fuel. It is important to use ox kidney for this, not lamb or anything more expensive, as the ox kidney gives the dish its flavour. The quantities given will feed six to eight people, and any leftovers can be heated and used again.*

Soak the beans overnight in plenty of cold water, drain them, and put them in a large saucepan covered with fresh cold water. Bring to the boil and boil for twenty minutes. In the meantime, skin the kidney and cut it into small pieces and soak it in warm salted water while the beans are boiling. Heat the olive oil in a frying pan, and gently fry the sliced onions, carrots and garlic. Drain the kidney and add it to the pan. Season with salt, pepper and a sprinkling of allspice and stir for a few minutes. Have ready a big ovenproof pot (about 5 pint or 3 litres capacity) and put half the drained beans in. Then add the kidney mixture. Put a big bunch of herbs on top of the meat, and add the rest of the beans. Then put in about 1½ pints (900 ml.) hot water or stock and a little more salt. Cover with greaseproof paper and the lid. Cook in a cool oven (Gas mark 1, Electric 275°F., 140°C.) for about 5 hours, and stir in the mustard thoroughly before serving. As long as you keep the oven very low, there is little danger of overcooking this dish. It is substantial enough for a one-course meal, but you can offer fresh fruit afterwards.

1 lb. (500 g.) haricot beans

1½ lb. (750 g.) ox kidney

4 tablespoons olive oil

2 onions

2 large carrots

Salt, freshly milled pepper, ground allspice

A bunch of parsley stalks, bayleaves and thyme

2 cloves garlic

2 teaspoons strong made mustard

Beef stock (if you have any)

# Ox Kidney with Mushrooms

*A very attractive looking dish, and an excellent way of dealing with tough kidneys. You can use port instead of wine, if you happen to have some. Very small new potatoes, scrubbed and boiled in their skins go very well with this, or very creamy mashed potatoes, with a little lemon thyme mixed in. The quantities given are ample for four people.*

1 lb. (500 g.) ox kidneys
½ lb. (250 g.) mushrooms
1 small glass red wine
1 clove garlic
Chopped parsley
1 oz. (30 g.) butter
½ oz. (15 g.) flour
Salt and black pepper

Soak the kidneys in warm salted water for about 2 hours. Cut them into slices about ¼ in. thick, salt and pepper them and roll them in the flour. Melt the butter in a frying pan and sauté the kidneys. Pour in the red wine, let it bubble for about 1 minute, and then add enough water to just cover the kidneys. Cover and stew very gently for about 1 hour. Unless the mushrooms are very large, wash them and leave them whole, and add them to the kidneys. Add the garlic, and simmer for another ½ hour without a lid. Sprinkle with a little chopped parsley before serving.

# Grilled Pig's Kidneys

*A very quick and tasty meal and, if you are careful about splitting and skewering the kidneys, they can look very attractive. If you use pig's kidneys, one is sufficient for each person, but you should allow two lamb's kidneys each.*

2 pig's kidneys
Oil
Salt and pepper
Maître d'hotel butter (See page 175)
Parsley
One slice of toast for each kidney

Split the kidneys with a sharp knife, leaving them joined at the flattest side, and remove the core and skin. Carefully thread a skewer through them to keep them flat. Brush them with oil and sprinkle them well with salt and pepper. Grill them until they are brown on both sides, then reduce the heat and continue cooking them until they are tender — this takes about 10 minutes. Serve them on toast with a pat of maître d'hotel butter on top, and garnished with plenty of fresh parsley.

# Pig's Trotters

Pig's trotters (or feet) are usually extremely cheap, a matter of a few pence each. Well cooked, they can be very good and lovely jelly is produced in the preliminary boiling. If the trotters are small, allow two per person, otherwise one is usually enough. Ask the butcher to split them lengthways for you.

# Pig's Trotters Sainte Ménéhould

*A rather elaborate method of dealing with simple pig's feet, but the result is delicious. You should tie the trotters together in twos, so that they do not fall to pieces in the cooking.*

1 or 2 feet per person
    (depending on the size)
Boiling water
Small glass white wine
1 teaspoon vinegar
1 onion, stuck with 4 cloves
2 baby carrots
1 leek
A good branch of thyme
2 bayleaves
3 black peppercorns
Salt (if the trotters have not
    been salted)
Melted dripping
Fine breadcrumbs

If the trotters have been salted, soak them overnight. Drain, and tie them. Put boiling water into a large pan, and add all the other ingredients. Let them simmer for about 3 hours very slowly — the surface of the liquid should be just barely moving. When tender, drain them and leave them to get cold. Strain the liquid and put it into a bowl for use in stocks and soups, etc. Untie the trotters, remove the bones or not, as you wish, and dip the pieces in melted dripping. Coat them thoroughly with fine breadcrumbs and brown them evenly under the grill. Serve hot with creamy mashed potatoes, and mustard or tartare sauce.

# Trotters with White Sauce

4 trotters

2 onions

Pinch ground mace

Piece lemon rind

1 pint (600 ml.) white stock

½ oz. (15 g.) flour

Salt and black pepper

Chopped parsley

Put the trotters, sliced onions, mace and lemon rind in a saucepan with the stock and simmer for 2 hours. Remove the trotters and keep them hot. Blend the flour smoothly with a little cold water, and thicken the liquid in the pan with it. Boil gently for 2 or 3 minutes. Pour the sauce over the trotters and serve hot sprinkled with parsley. A few chopped capers sprinkled over are also good.

# Jellied Pig's Feet

2 or 3 trotters

Salt

A bunch of herbs

A blade of mace

1 slice of onion

1 small carrot

1 dessertspoon chopped parsley

Wash the feet and blanch them. Put them into a saucepan with all the other ingredients, except the parsley. Just cover with cold water and allow to simmer until the meat is tender (about 2 hours). Remove the trotters and strain the liquid. Remove meat from the bones and dice it. Stir into the stock with the parsley, pour into a wet mould or basin, and leave in a cold place to set.

# Tête de Boeuf Farci

*Ox cheek is a very economical buy, and has a delicious flavour. It should be cooked slowly, and is extremely good in stews. Butchers often sell it cut up, but for the following recipe you must get the cheek in one piece.*

If the cheek has not already been boned, bone it and let it soak in cold water overnight. Wash it well in warm water, and when it is thoroughly clean, dry it and spread it out on a board. Season it well with salt and pepper.

To make the stuffing:
Put the breadcrumbs into a basin, add the suet and the chopped parsley and ham, the grated lemon rind and the mixed herbs. Mix thoroughly, season with pepper and salt and bind with the egg or milk. Spread the stuffing over the cheek, roll it up and tie it securely with string or tape. Melt a little dripping in the bottom of a deep casserole, and add the diced vegetables to a depth of about 2 ins. Season with salt and pepper and add a bunch of fresh herbs. Put in the prepared meat, put the lid on the casserole and cook for ¼ hour, shaking the pan to prevent sticking. Then pour enough stock (and wine) in to cover the vegetables, replace the lid and cook for about four hours very slowly, either on top of the cooker or in a very slow oven (Gas mark 1, Electric 275°F., 140°C.). Baste the meat fairly frequently or it will become dry. When it is cooked, take it from the casserole and allow it to brown for a few minutes. Strain the stock and reduce it by boiling. Remove the string or tape from the meat and put it on a hot serving dish. Serve it with the reduced stock poured over, and garnished with small whole baked tomatoes.
Sufficient for 4 to 6 people.

1 ox cheek
Herb stuffing:
¼ lb. (120 g.) breadcrumbs
2 tablespoons chopped suet (or
    2 tablespoons melted butter)
1 dessertspoon chopped parsley
Grated rind ½ lemon
1 oz. (30 g.) chopped ham
    (optional)
½ teaspoon powdered mixed herbs
Salt and pepper
Beaten egg or milk to bind
Stock and a small glass white wine
    (optional)
Vegetables for braising:
Carrot, turnip, } in equal
Onion, celery } proportions
1 tomato
1 leek
Tomatoes for garnishing

# Pork Brawn

*There are many recipes for brawn to be found but this one, from a collection of recipes produced by the Scottish Women's Rural Institutes during the post war period of food rationing, is very good — simple to prepare and extraordinarily cheap.*

Wash the pig's head in tepid water. Remove the brains and the eyes. Take out any splinters of bone and clean the head thoroughly. Blanch it in boiling water to cleanse and whiten it. Rinse it well, cover with cold water and simmer for 2 hours. When the meat is sufficiently tender, remove it from the bones and cut into dice. Put the bones back into the liquor in which the head was boiled, add the seasonings and the onion, bring to the boil and simmer for about 1 hour. Strain the liquor and add about 2 pints (1.2 litres) of it to the prepared meat with plenty of pepper and salt. Rinse a mould or basin with cold water and pour in the meat and liquor. Leave to set, turn out and serve garnished with sliced gherkins, parsley, and any other pickles you have.

If you want to include the brains, wash them thoroughly when you remove them from the head and tie them in muslin — they can then be cooked in the same pan as the head. When you are preparing the rest of the meat, remove the brains from the muslin and cut them into neat pieces and mix them with the rest of the meat. The tongue should be skinned before it is diced.

Half a pig's head

1 blade mace

12 allspice

1 onion

20 peppercorns

4 cloves

Bunch of herbs (parsley, thyme, marjoram, bay)

# Lamb's Tongues with Lemon Sauce

1 lb. (500 g.) lamb's tongues
1 stick celery
1 teaspoon chopped parsley
1 carrot
½ onion
1 oz. (30 g.) butter
1 tablespoon flour
1 teaspoon sugar
Juice and grated rind of 1 lemon

Soak the tongues in salted water for 2 hours. Rinse and put them in a pan of cold water. Bring to the boil then rinse them in fresh water again. Place in a pan with celery, carrot, onion and parsley, cover with water and stew until tender. Skin the tongues and cut them in two lengthwise. Melt the butter, stir in flour and gradually add the sugar, lemon rind and juice, with ½ pint (300 ml.) of the strained tongue broth. Bring to the boil, stirring all the time, then add the tongues to the sauce and simmer gently for about 10 minutes.

# Ox Tongue

1 ox tongue
1 lb. (500 g.) block salt
6 oz. (180 g.) brown sugar
1 oz. (30 g.) saltpetre
1 gallon (5 litres) water

*To pickle an ox tongue:*
Wash and scrape the tongue thoroughly to remove all the slimy substance and rinse it in cold water. Remove the gristle and root part, and rub the tongue all over with coarse salt. Leave it overnight to drain.

Prepare the pickle as follows:
Boil together for 5 minutes the salt, brown sugar, saltpetre and water. Skim the surface, strain the pickle into a large bowl and leave to get cold. Pour the pickle over the tongue, making sure that it is completely covered and leave it for one week.

1 pickled ox tongue

1 onion

1 carrot

1 piece turnip

2 stalks celery

2 bay leaves

6 peppercorns

Bunch fresh herbs

*To cook a pickled ox tongue* (either pickled by the butcher or yourself):

Soak the pickled tongue in cold water overnight. Wash it well in cold water. Bring some water to boil in a large pan, put in the tongue and simmer for ½ hour. Throw the water away and replace it with fresh, cold water. Add the rest of the ingredients. Bring to the boil and allow to simmer gently until the tongue is tender (about ½ hour per lb. [1 hour per kilogram]). When the tongue is cooked, remove it from the pan and plunge it into cold water. Put it on a dish and remove the thick skin, and bones in the root, and any remaining fat and gristle.

*To serve the tongue hot:*

Put the tongue on a fireproof dish and slice it. Pour over some Polish sauce (see page 176) or caper sauce (see page 177), and reheat it in a moderate oven (Gas mark 5, Electric 375ºF., 190ºC.) for 15–20 minutes. Very good served with spinach purée.

*To serve the tongue cold:*

Trim the cooked tongue, roll it into a round shape and put it into a cake tin. Make sure that it is a very tight fit in the tin and pour in a little of the strained liquor in which it was cooked to fill any crevices. Cover with a plate that just fits inside the tin and put a heavy weight on top. Leave to get quite cold and then turn out. Garnish with plenty of water-cress.

If you have any tongue left over, mince it and mix it with a little Espagnole sauce (see page 176), and a little chopped ham or bacon. You can then use it as a filling for a savoury flan.

# Oxtail with White Grapes

*This is a really delicious stew, but of course, you should only attempt it when grapes are plentiful and cheap — those small seedless ones are ideal, and for a short time they are usually very reasonably priced. This dish takes a long time to cook so it is worth saving it for a time when you have a lot of people to feed — the following quantities will serve serve eight people.*

2 oxtails, cut into pieces by
   the butcher
3 oz. (90 g.) fat unsmoked bacon,
   in one piece
2 large onions
4 large carrots
2 lb. (1 kg.) white grapes
Salt and freshly ground black
   pepper
A pinch ground mace
*Bouquet garni* (2 bayleaves,
   parsley, thyme)
2 cloves garlic, crushed

Soak the tail in cold water for two hours, drain and dry. Remove the rind from the bacon and dice it. Have ready a heavy cooking pot which can be used both on top of the cooker and in the oven. Put the bacon in the bottom of the pot with the chopped vegetables on top. Cook slowly on a low heat for 10 minutes until the bacon fat starts to run. Put in the pieces of oxtail, and the *bouquet* and garlic. Season, cover the pot and cook gently for about 20 minutes. Remove the stalks from the grapes and crush them slightly in a bowl. Add them to the meat. Cover the pot with two layers of greaseproof paper and the lid. Put in a very slow oven (Gas mark 1, Electric 275°F., 140°C.) and cook for at least 3½ hours. When the meat is so tender that it is almost falling off the bone, remove it with some of the pieces of bacon and put them in a serving dish to keep hot. Sieve the rest of the ingredients, and pour the resulting sauce over the oxtail. Serve with jacket potatoes.

# Cow Heel with Parsley Sauce

*Another very economical buy, and worth the rather lengthy preparation.*

Wash and scrape the heel and cut it into four pieces. Remove the fat from between the hoof pieces. Put these into a saucepan with cold water to cover

them, bring them to the boil and pour the water
away, rinsing the pan and the heel well to get rid
of all scum. Cover the heel with fresh cold water
and bring it to the boil. Skim if necessary and then
add the onions and fresh herbs. Cover the pan and
simmer until tender (2 − 3 hours). Check every so
often to make sure that the water does not boil
away. When tender, drain the heel and reserve the
liquid. Prepare the sauce by melting the butter in a
pan. Stir in the flour, and when it is smooth pour
in ½ pint (300 ml.) of the liquid from the cow heel
and stir until boiling. Season to taste and stir in
1 tablespoon chopped parsley, and a little milk if
you think the sauce is too thick. Remove the meat
from the bones, and serve it on a hot dish with the
sauce poured over. Polish Sauce (see page 176) or
caper sauce (see page 177) are also good with cow
heel.

1 cow heel
2 onions
A bunch of fresh herbs
1 oz. (30 g.) butter
1 oz. (30 g.) flour
1 tablespoon chopped parsley
Milk

# Chicken

Chicken used to be a treat for a special occasion,
but now it has become one of the most economical
and useful foods available. It is now cheaper than
prime meat and even those incredibly hard frozen
birds can be delicious as long as you thaw them
very slowly and thoroughly. I find that these frozen
birds are very good if they are roasted in an earthenware chicken 'brick' with herbs and vegetables. And
frozen chicken joints can be successfully fried, if
they are coated with a well-seasoned flour and
breadcrumb mixture — this makes a very good meal
served with sweet corn and watercress. If you find
that your chicken is a bit elderly and therefore
fatty, do not throw away the fat — render it down
and use it for frying where you might otherwise
use butter (see page 173).

# Chicken Stew

*Use an old bird for this recipe, and use its own fat for frying.*

1 boiling fowl, jointed into 6–8
    pieces
4 oz. (120 g.) chicken fat (or
    pork dripping)
Flour, seasoned with salt and
    pepper
2 large, sliced onions
½ lb. (250 g.) tomatoes,
    quartered
6 green olives (optional)
2 bay leaves
¼ teaspoon mixed herbs
1 tablespoon flour
1 teaspoon salt
¼ teaspoon pepper
4 oz. (120 g.) mushrooms,
    washed and sliced

Take a heavy, deep saucepan and heat the fat or dripping. Coat the chicken joints in the seasoned flour and brown them on all sides in the fat. Remove the chicken from the pan and keep it hot. Put the onions, olives and tomatoes into the pan, and fry for 5 minutes, stirring. Add the bay leaves and herbs, sprinkle in the tablespoon of flour and the salt and pepper and stir well. Put in the chicken and add sufficient water, or stock, to cover. Simmer with the lid on for about 2 hours, or until the meat is tender. Twenty minutes before the chicken is cooked, add the mushrooms and continue to simmer. Arrange the joints in the centre of a serving dish and arrange the vegetables around. Thicken the sauce with a little flour, and pour it over the chicken.

# Boiling Chicken with Rice

1 boiling chicken
A bunch of herbs (parsley, thyme,
    marjoram, and bay)
Salt and 6 black peppercorns
3 onions
1 slice belly pork
2 cloves
½ lb. (250 g.) rice

Put the chicken into a deep saucepan and cover with hot water. Add all the ingredients, except the rice. Cook gently for about 1½ – 2 hours, then lift out the chicken, add the rice to the stock, and put the chicken back on top of the rice. Reduce the heat, cover the pan, and continue to simmer gently until the rice is cooked and most of the liquid is absorbed.

# Chicken Pilaff

*This recipe uses cold cooked chicken — perhaps leftovers from a roast chicken.*

1 large onion
2 tablespoons olive oil
6 oz. (180 g.) long grain rice
¾ pint (450 ml.) chicken stock
1 teaspoon salt
¼ teaspoon freshly ground
    black pepper
¼ teaspoon mixed herbs
2 oz. (60 g.) seedless raisins
1 tablespoon chopped cucumber
12 oz. (360 g.) chopped cooked
    chicken
1 tinned red pepper

Chop the onion finely and fry it in the oil until it is transparent. Wash the rice, dry it and add it to the onion. Fry gently for 5 minutes, stirring all the time. Add the stock, the seasoning and the herbs, the raisins and the chopped cucumber. Cover and simmer gently for about 20 minutes, or until the rice is tender and the liquid has been absorbed, stirring from time to time. Stir in the chopped chicken and taste to see if more seasoning is needed. Serve on a hot dish, garnished with the pepper cut into strips, or with tomato if no pepper is available.

# Devilled Chicken

*Another recipe using cold, cooked chicken — very good if you have to produce a meal in a hurry as you could even buy a ready-cooked bird, although it would be more economical to cook it yourself.*

Cooked chicken
For devilled dressing:
A dash of cayenne pepper
½ teaspoon black pepper
1 teaspoon piquant sauce
    (e.g. Worcester Sauce)
1 teaspoon made mustard
1 teaspoon vinegar
2 dessertspoons oil

Cut the chicken into neat pieces, removing any skin and surplus fat. Blend all the ingredients for the dressing, and brush over the pieces of chicken. Cook under a hot grill, turning the pieces until they are nicely browned. Serve at once.

# Chicken with Cream and Cheese Sauce

*Yet another use for cold left-over chicken, or even turkey. The following quantities will serve four people. The cream gives the dish a luxury touch which makes it very suitable for a dinner party, and it is worth using Parmesan or Gruyère if you possibly can. A truly delicious meal.*

¾ lb. (360 g.) cooked chicken,
    cut into small thin strips
1½ oz. (45 g.) butter
2 heaped tablespoons flour
½ pint (300 ml.) milk
4 tablespoons stock
4 tablespoons cream
Salt and freshly milled pepper
Nutmeg
3 tablespoons grated Parmesan
    or Gruyère
Breadcrumbs

Melt the butter in a thick saucepan, add the flour and stir it, off the heat, until it forms a smooth paste. Then add a little of the warmed milk. Return to the heat and stir in the rest of the milk. When the sauce is really smooth and thick add the cream, the stock and the seasonings — do not add very much salt at this stage. Now put the pan containing the sauce into another larger one containing water, and let it cook in this double pan for about 20 minutes, stirring it frequently. Add the cheese and stir until it is fully amalgamated; taste the sauce to see if more salt is required. Cover the bottom of a shallow fireproof dish with a thin layer of the sauce. Put in the chicken and cover it completely with the rest of the sauce. Sprinkle the top with breadcrumbs and a little more grated cheese. Cook for about 15 minutes in a moderate oven (Gas mark 4, Electric 350ºF., 180ºC.) and then put it under a very hot grill for a couple of minutes, so that the top starts to bubble.

# Turkey

Like chicken, turkey is no longer a luxury meat — in fact, at certain times it is one of the cheapest meats available in terms of price per pound. I will not give a recipe for roasting a whole turkey, but it is fairly common practice now to sell drumsticks separately and these are sufficiently meaty to provide a very good meal.

# Stuffed Turkey Drumsticks

Remove the bones and tendons from the drumsticks without breaking the skin, then fill the cavity in each with forcemeat or sausagemeat, keeping the original shape of the drumstick. Fasten the opening with a small skewer, or some string. Put the drumsticks into a greased fireproof dish, add enough stock to come half-way up, and bake in a moderate oven (Gas mark 5, Electric 375°F., 190°C.), for about 1 hour, or until the meat is tender.

# Devilled Turkey Legs

Cooked turkey legs can be devilled in the same way as chicken (see page 105).

# Savoury Turkey Border

*A good way of using up cold turkey — a problem that most people are faced with after Christmas.*

Cut ½ lb. (250 g.) turkey meat into small pieces and season it well. Melt 1 oz. (30 g.) butter or margarine in a pan, add 1 oz. (30 g.) flour, cook for a few minutes, stirring all the time. Add 1 rasher of bacon, chopped, 3 chopped olives, 1 finely chopped fried onion and some very thin slices of green pepper. Cook over a low heat, until the pepper is cooked, then stir in the meat and a little lemon juice and heat thoroughly. Taste to see if more seasoning is needed, and stir in one egg yolk. Serve piled in the middle of a border of mashed potatoes.

# Turkey Cigars

*A variation on rissoles or croquettes.*

1 oz. (30 g.) butter or margarine

1 oz. (30 g.) flour

½ pint (300 ml.) stock

Salt and pepper

Lemon juice

4 oz. (120 g.) minced cooked
   turkey

2 oz. (60 g.) minced ham

1 oz. (30 g.) minced mushrooms

1 teaspoon top of the milk

Egg for coating

Breadcrumbs

Oil for frying

Melt the butter or margarine, stir in the flour and gradually add the stock, stirring all the time. Bring to the boil, season and add a dash of lemon juice. Stir in the turkey, ham, mushrooms and milk, and leave to cool. When cool enough to handle, form the mixture into cigar shapes. Brush them with beaten egg, coat with breadcrumbs, and fry in smoking hot oil until golden-brown. The cigars can be served hot with a good sauce, and vegetables, or may be eaten cold with salad.

# Rabbit

Rabbit has always been a favourite of mine, bringing back childhood memories of magnificent rabbit pies baked by my mother. Some people find it dry and insipid, but cooked with care and imagination it is neither of these things. I do not honestly believe that there is a great deal of difference in flavour between wild and tame animals, but if the price difference is very small, then buy wild. You can usually buy rabbit whole or ask the butcher to joint it for you. It is not very difficult to joint — and you have more control over the number of pieces if you joint it yourself.

# Maryland Rabbit

Joint the rabbit and soak the joints in salted water for about 1 hour. Rinse and dry the joints. Sprinkle the rabbit with salt and pepper and rub it well in. Dip them in flour, then in the beaten egg which

1 rabbit

4 oz. (120 g.) pork dripping or lard

Salt and pepper

A little flour

1 beaten egg

2–3 oz. (60–90 g.) fine white
   breadcrumbs

you have diluted with 2 teaspoons water. Allow any surplus egg to drip off, and then toss the joints in breadcrumbs. Heat the fat in a frying pan and lightly brown the joints all over. Transfer the joints to a casserole, add the fat from the pan, cover them with foil, and then put the lid on. Bake for about 45 minutes in a hot oven (Gas mark 6, Electric 400°F., 200°C.), basting from time to time. Serve with a good savoury sauce (e.g. onion sauce, see page 177).

# Creamed Rabbit

1 rabbit

*Bouquet garni* (dried mixed herbs,
   bay leaf, blade of mace, sprig
   of parsley and a few peppercorns tied in muslin)

1 carrot

1 small onion

Salt

¾ pint (450 ml.) stock

2 oz. (60 g.) butter

2 oz. (60 g.) flour

¼ pint (150 ml.) milk

A pinch of powdered mace

2 tablespoons top of the milk

Garnish:

Baked or grilled tomatoes

Baked or grilled mushrooms

Bacon rolls

Dry boiled rice

Wash the rabbit and soak it in salted water for about two hours. Joint it. Put it in a saucepan with the *bouquet garni,* carrot, onion, salt and enough stock to cover. Simmer gently until the rabbit is tender. Drain the rabbit and keep it hot. Strain the liquid – you will need about ¾ pint (450 ml.) for the sauce. Melt the butter, add the flour and blend it well. Stir in the milk and the hot stock and stir until boiling. Season to taste, add a pinch of powdered mace and the top of the milk. The sauce should be of a creamy texture. Pour the sauce over the rabbit and serve it garnished with tomatoes, mushrooms, bacon rolls and rice.

# Rabbit à l'Italienne

*A very tasty dish, and as it uses pasta you will not need to serve any other vegetables — simply a nice green salad to follow.*

2 or 3 onions
1 oz. (30 g.) mushrooms
Oil for frying
1 rabbit, jointed
A little vinegar
1 oz. (30 g.) flour
Salt and black pepper
Stock
4 oz. (120 g.) macaroni or spaghetti
½ lb. (250 g.) tomatoes
1 oz. (30 g.) grated cheese

Slice the onions and mushrooms and fry them in a little hot oil for a few minutes. Dip the rabbit joints in vinegar and then in seasoned flour, add them to the onion mixture and fry till golden brown. Just cover with stock (or water) and simmer gently for about 1 hour, or until the rabbit is tender. Cook the pasta in the usual way. About 5 minutes before the rabbit is cooked, add the tomatoes to the stew — let them soften, but do not let them break up. Put the rabbit on a hot dish, pile drained pasta at either end, and garnish with the whole tomatoes, the onions and mushrooms. Sprinkle with grated cheese. Thicken the sauce slightly with a little flour, and serve it separately.

# Rabbit and Lentils

*A very good dish from the Mediterranean.*

1 rabbit
2 rashers of bacon
Oil for sautéeing
1 glass cider (or white wine)
Salt and freshly ground black
    pepper
Good bunch fresh herbs
For the lentil purée:
1 lb. (500 g.) brown lentils
1 onion stuck with 2 cloves
2 cloves garlic
2 carrots
Salt

Cut the rabbit into large pieces, chop the bacon, and sauté the rabbit and bacon in the oil. Pour over the cider and let it bubble for a minute or two. Add the seasoning and the herbs, cover the pan, and simmer gently until the rabbit is tender. In the meantime, prepare a purée of lentils:

Put the lentils, the onion, the garlic, carrots and salt into a pan and cover with water. Simmer for 2 hours, remove the vegetables and sieve the lentils. Mix the liquid from the rabbit into the purée, add the rabbit and the bacon, and reheat.

# Rabbit Pie

*This recipe, from Derbyshire, produces one of the best pies I have tasted.*

8 oz. (250 g.) shortcrust pastry
¼ lb. (120 g.) sausage meat,
    rolled into balls
1 rabbit, jointed
6 rashers of bacon
2 teaspoons chopped parsley
1 or 2 hard-boiled eggs
1 small onion
1 teaspoon flour
Salt and pepper
Pinch of nutmeg
A little stock

Roll out the pastry to fit the top of the pie dish. Mix the flour with the salt, pepper and nutmeg, and dip the pieces of rabbit in it. Line the dish with the bacon, and arrange the rabbit, parsley, onion and sliced eggs in layers. Add a little stock and cover with pastry, with a pie funnel in the middle. If you have a few scraps of pastry left, you can make leaves to decorate the top of the pie. Put into a hot oven (Gas mark 7, Electric 425°F., 220°C.) for 5 minutes, then reduce the heat to Gas mark 4, Electric 350°F., 180°C., and bake for 1½ hours. Pour a little more stock down the funnel and bake for a further ten minutes. The sausage meat balls are optional and, if used, should be added before the pastry lid is put on. If the pastry seems to be getting too brown, you can cover it with greaseproof paper.

# Marble Rabbit

*A cold rabbit mould, very good served with a potato salad.*

Joint a rabbit and put it into a casserole just covered with water. Add a glass of white wine, an onion stuck with 2 cloves, and a carrot. Season well, cover and stew in the oven until the meat is tender, and coming off the bone. Leave to cool and remove the meat from the bone, cutting it into neat pieces. Add ½ oz. (15 g.) gelatine to the strained stock, put the rabbit into a wetted mould or basin, and pour the liquor over it. Leave to set, and turn out when required.

# Stuffed Baked Rabbit

*The quantities given here will feed four people — baked jacket potatoes and cabbage, cauliflower or sprouts are a good accompaniment. Add bread sauce (see page 175), and you have a fine meal at very low cost.*

Stuff the rabbit with the sage and onion stuffing, and stitch up the opening with coarse thread. Put it into a baking tin containing water about 1 in. deep. Peel the onions, but do not slice them, and add them to the pan. Sprinkle a little flour on the rabbit and cover it with the rashers. Season well with pepper and salt, and cover the whole pan with greaseproof paper. Bake for ½ an hour in a hot oven (Gas mark 7, Electric 425°F., 220°C.). Then remove the paper and continue to cook until the meat is tender, basting frequently. Thicken the liquid in the pan with a little flour and serve it with the rabbit.

1 rabbit
Sage and onion stuffing
    (see page 172)
Salt and pepper
2 or 3 rashers of fat bacon
3 or 4 medium sized onions

# Flemish Rabbit

*A rather strange dish — fairly rich and heavy, and best accompanied by plain, boiled rice.*

Melt 1 oz. (30 g.) butter in a heavy saucepan, cut the pork into thin strips and brown them lightly. Remove the pork and keep hot. Now brown the rabbit pieces all over in the same butter, remove and keep with the pork. Brown the onions. Return everything to the saucepan and sprinkle in 1 level tablespoon flour. Stir well and pour in the cider. Add the salt, pepper, thyme and simmer with a lid on for 1 hour. Add the raisins, sultanas and prunes and simmer for another hour. Put 3 tablespoons sugar into a small pan with one tablespoon vinegar and heat it until it just starts to caramelize. Stir this well into the rabbit sauce and serve at once.

4 pieces of rabbit
¼ lb. (120 g.) belly pork or fat
    bacon
¼ lb. (120 g.) mixed sultanas
    and raisins
8 small onions
6 prunes
1 pint (600 ml.) cider or water
Vinegar
Flour, butter
Salt, pepper and sugar
A little thyme

# Fricassée of Rabbit

1 rabbit
¼ lb. (120 g.) streaky bacon
Bouquet of herbs
A blade of mace
A large onion stuck with 3 cloves
Salt
2 oz. (60 g.) butter
1 tablespoon flour
8 small onions
1 glass white wine
2 egg yolks
Nutmeg
Sliced lemon
Toast

Joint the rabbit and wash it in salted water. Drain it, and put it into a saucepan with the chopped bacon, the herbs, the mace, the onion, and a little salt. Cover with cold water, bring to the boil, and simmer for 20 minutes, skimming off any scum. Drain off the liquid through a sieve, and keep it hot. Using a clean saucepan, melt the butter, and stir in the flour. Add some of the liquid and stir well until it thickens. Add the rabbit, bacon, and small onions and simmer until the onions are soft. Mix the wine with the egg yolks, add a little grated nutmeg, and beat well. Pour this into the stew and stir carefully until it thickens. Take out the rabbit and arrange it on a hot serving dish. Pour the sauce over, and serve garnished with slices of lemon and squares of toast.

# Baked Rabbit

1 rabbit, jointed
3—4 medium onions, boiled and
    chopped
1 heaped cup breadcrumbs
2 oz. (60 g.) dripping
Salt and pepper
Sage

*A wartime special, this one — when rabbit was a welcome addition to the meat ration.*

Make a paste with the breadcrumbs, the onions, salt and pepper, a little dried sage and about 1 oz. (30 g.) of melted dripping. Melt a little more dripping in a baking tin and spread half the paste on it. Arrange the rabbit joints on top of this and cover them with the rest of the mixture. Bake in a moderate oven (Gas mark 4, Electric 350°F., 180°C.) for about 1½ hours. If the rabbit is a fairly old one, cook it at Gas mark 3, Electric 325°F., 170°C. for about 2 hours. As long as the rabbit is well covered by the paste, it will not be at all dry.

# Farmhouse Rabbit

*A dish to cook when broad beans and peas are readily available. It can be served hot or cold.*

1 rabbit, jointed

1½ lb. (750 g.) young broad beans

1 leek

½ lb. (250 g.) green peas

2 potatoes

Butter

Vinaigrette sauce (made with
    olive oil, lemon, a little garlic,
    and chopped herbs, including
    lemon thyme, if possible)

Hard-boiled eggs
    (optional)

Season the rabbit well with salt and pepper. Melt the butter in a large pan, and brown the rabbit gently all over. Add the shelled peas, the leek and potatoes cut in pieces, and the beans in their pods, if they are young enough. Only the black end of the pods near the stalk need be cut off, but if the beans are too old to be cooked in this way, you will have to use more. Add sufficient water to just cover the vegetables, season with salt and pepper (and 3 lumps of sugar), and cook fairly slowly for about 1½ hours. Remove the pieces of rabbit and pour the vinaigrette sauce over them while they are still hot. Sieve the vegetables so that you have a thick puree (keep the liquid for stock). Pile the puree in the middle of a shallow dish with the pieces of rabbit arranged all round. Serve cold, garnished with quartered hard-boiled eggs, if you wish. If you want to serve this as a hot dish, do not pour a vinaigrette sauce over the rabbit joints when you remove them from the pan — instead, sprinkle them with salt and pepper and pour a little oil on them. Then fry them gently or heat them under the grill while you reheat the purée.

# Vegetables

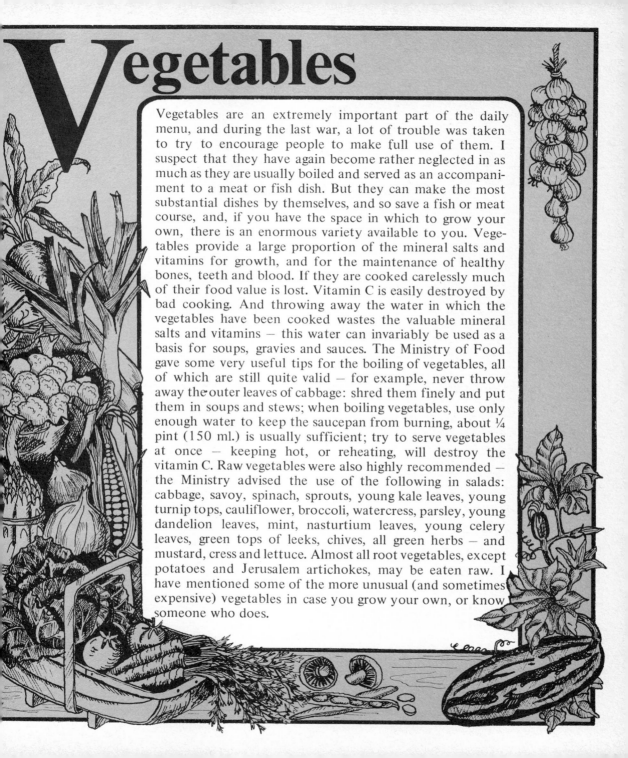

Vegetables are an extremely important part of the daily menu, and during the last war, a lot of trouble was taken to try to encourage people to make full use of them. I suspect that they have again become rather neglected in as much as they are usually boiled and served as an accompaniment to a meat or fish dish. But they can make the most substantial dishes by themselves, and so save a fish or meat course, and, if you have the space in which to grow your own, there is an enormous variety available to you. Vegetables provide a large proportion of the mineral salts and vitamins for growth, and for the maintenance of healthy bones, teeth and blood. If they are cooked carelessly much of their food value is lost. Vitamin C is easily destroyed by bad cooking. And throwing away the water in which the vegetables have been cooked wastes the valuable mineral salts and vitamins — this water can invariably be used as a basis for soups, gravies and sauces. The Ministry of Food gave some very useful tips for the boiling of vegetables, all of which are still quite valid — for example, never throw away the outer leaves of cabbage: shred them finely and put them in soups and stews; when boiling vegetables, use only enough water to keep the saucepan from burning, about ¼ pint (150 ml.) is usually sufficient; try to serve vegetables at once — keeping hot, or reheating, will destroy the vitamin C. Raw vegetables were also highly recommended — the Ministry advised the use of the following in salads: cabbage, savoy, spinach, sprouts, young kale leaves, young turnip tops, cauliflower, broccoli, watercress, parsley, young dandelion leaves, mint, nasturtium leaves, young celery leaves, green tops of leeks, chives, all green herbs — and mustard, cress and lettuce. Almost all root vegetables, except potatoes and Jerusalem artichokes, may be eaten raw. I have mentioned some of the more unusual (and sometimes expensive) vegetables in case you grow your own, or know someone who does.

# Artichokes, Globe

Wash them, and boil them in salted water, with a little lemon juice, for ½ hour. Serve them cold with oil and lemon, or hot with melted butter.

# Artichokes, Jerusalem

A winter vegetable, which is very easy to grow. A little fiddly to peel; some people prefer to part cook them and then peel them. They take about 15 minutes to boil, and it is best to allow ½ lb. (250 g.) per person.

# Jerusalem Artichokes en Daube

*This is a delicious dish — but be careful not to overcook the artichokes, or they will turn to purée.*

2 lb. (1 kg.) artichokes
2 small onions
1 tablespoon flour
A little oil or beef dripping
A small glass white wine (or cider)
1 clove garlic, crushed
Black pepper and salt
Pinch ground nutmeg

Slice the onions and brown them in the oil. Sprinkle in the flour and stir until it is golden. Add the wine or cider, let it bubble for a minute, and then put in the artichokes, which you have peeled. (Small artichokes are best.) Add the salt, pepper, nutmeg, and the garlic, and just enough water to cover. Simmer gently for about 15 minutes, or until the artichokes are cooked. Stir in a good tablespoon of chopped parsley before serving.

# Jerusalem Artichoke Soufflé

¼ pint (150 ml.) artichoke purée
¼ pint (150 ml.) milk
2 eggs
Grated lemon rind
Salt and pepper

Cook and drain some artichokes and sieve them until you have about ¼ pint (150 ml.) purée. Beat the yolks of the eggs with the milk and strain them into the purée. Season with salt, pepper and a little grated lemon rind. Whip the egg whites stiffly and stir them lightly into the artichoke mixture. Pour into a well-greased soufflé dish, and bake in a moderate oven (Gas mark 4, Electric 350ºF., 180ºC.) for 20–30 minutes, until well-risen and firm to the touch. Serve at once. You can cook this in four individual soufflé dishes if you have them.

# Asparagus

It is not absolutely necessary to throw away the thick stalks of asparagus – during the war, it was recommended that these be peeled very thinly, so that they could be eaten. Also, the peelings should be kept for soup. To cook it, tie the pieces together in bundles, and stand them upright in a deep pan of boiling water, to which you have added salt, as well as a lump of sugar. The heads should be above the water level so that they are cooked by the steam. Small asparagus will take about 15 minutes to cook, and larger stalks about ½ hour. Serve it with melted butter, or oil and lemon.

# Aubergines

It is possible to grow these at home, either in a cool greenhouse or in a sun lounge, and at the height of their season it is sometimes possible to buy them fairly cheaply (in the autumn). Unless they are to be puréed or used in salad, it is best not to peel them. The skin holds them together while cooking, and also has a good flavour. Before cooking them, slice them into rounds, or lengths, or even into dice, put them into a colander and sprinkle them with salt. Press a plate down on top of them and leave them for about 2 hours. Of course, for some recipes they should be left whole.

# Aubergines en Gigot

In each whole, unpeeled aubergine, make two rows of small incisions. Cut the bacon into small pieces, also the garlic, and roll both in salt, pepper and herbs. Into the incisions in the aubergines put alternately pieces of bacon and pieces of garlic. Put the aubergines in a roasting tin or dish and pour a little oil over them. Cover them with foil and roast them in a slow oven (Gas mark 2, Electric 300°F., 150°C.) for about 1 hour. If you wish to serve them cold, leave them to get cold, carefully split them open, salt them and serve with a little fresh oil poured over.

1 aubergine per person
1 rasher of bacon per aubergine
Garlic
Salt and pepper
Marjoram or basil
A little oil

# Beans, Broad

A vegetable which has been used in this country longer than almost any other, it was long a source of protein for the poor, whose staple food was broad beans and boiled bacon. If the beans are very young, the pods can be eaten as well as the beans — the whole should be chopped into 1 in. pieces in the same way as French beans. To boil beans, drop them into boiling salted water to just cover, and boil gently for about 15 minutes.

# Boiled Bacon and Broad Beans

2 lbs. (1 kg.) boiling bacon
2 lbs. (1 kg.) broad beans

# Broad Beans with Ham

2 lb. (1 kg.) broad beans
Béchamel sauce (see page 46)
3 oz. (90 g.) single cream
2 oz. (60 g.) cooked ham
Chopped parsley

# Beans, French and Runner

*Use fresh young beans if possible, and accompany the dish with parsley sauce.*

Shell the broad beans and add them to the boiling bacon about 15 minutes before it should be cooked. Remove the bacon from the pan, skin it if you wish and put it on a hot serving dish with the beans arranged all around.

*This is a French version of the preceding recipe — a little more extravagant, but a wonderful dish.*

Shell the beans, boil them and strain them, keeping a little of the liquid. Make a béchamel, using the bean liquid instead of part of the milk. Stir in the cream, and then the ham, cut into strips. Add the beans, let them get thoroughly hot, stir in a little chopped parsley and serve. You can use salt pork or bacon instead of the ham, but the pork should be boiled before use, and the bacon fried until the fat starts to run.

Easy to grow if you have the space, and available in many varieties, including dwarf haricots, which can be allowed to mature and ripen for winter use. These beans are high in vitamin content and can be cooked in a variety of ways — a very good way of serving french beans (and also broad beans) is with an egg and lemon sauce: you simply boil the beans in the usual way and reserve about a cupful of the liquid. Whisk two eggs to a froth with the juice of the lemon, some olive oil, and a tablespoon of grated Parmesan. Add a little of the bean water, and heat this sauce over a low flame, whisking all the time until it starts to thicken. Pour it over the beans and serve either hot or cold.

## Runner Beans with Tomatoes

*You can use either scarlet runners or coarse French beans for this Provençal recipe.*

Top and tail the beans and string them if necessary. Break them into pieces and drop them into boiling salted water. Cook for 10 minutes and drain them. Heat 2 tablespoons of olive oil in a frying-pan, put in the beans, two or three tomatoes, skinned and roughly chopped, and a clove of garlic. Cook for 10 minutes gently, shaking the pan from time to time so that the beans do not stick. When the tomatoes have turned almost to a purée, remove the garlic, add a little chopped parsley, and serve at once.

## Green Beans with Spaghetti

½ lb. (250 g.) French beans,
   or young runners
3 oz. (90 g.) spaghetti
2 oz. (60 g.) butter
2 oz. (60 g.) grated cheese
Salt and black pepper
A red or green pepper, if available

Wash and string the beans if necessary, and cut them into thin strips. Drop them into boiling salted water and boil quickly for about 15 minutes, or until tender and remove any scum that rises. In the meantime, break the spaghetti into pieces, put it into a saucepan with warm water to cover, and add 1 oz. (30 g.) of the butter. Simmer slowly with a lid on until all the liquid is absorbed. Add the cheese and the seasoning, and shake over the heat for a few minutes. Drain the beans and shake the pan over the heat to dry them. Add the rest of the butter, some more seasoning, and shake to mix thoroughly. Chop the pepper and soften it in a little butter. Pile the beans in the centre of a hot dish. Sprinkle the pepper on top and arrange the spaghetti around to form a border.

## Beetroot

There are other things to do with beetroot apart from having them cold in salads. Again, if you grow your own, there are interesting varieties available such as golden and white beet, both of which have a higher food value than the usual dark red ones.

# Spiced Beetroot

Peel and slice a medium-sized onion and put it in a saucepan. Grate a large cooking apple over it and then grate in 1 lb. (500 g.) of boiled beetroots. Add two tablespoons brown sugar, 1 tablespoon ground cinnamon, 3 cloves, a pinch of salt and a knob of butter or margarine. Stir well and add about ½ cup of water. Cook very gently for about ¾ hour, stirring from time to time and serve very hot.

# Fricassée of Beetroot

Bake some beetroots slowly in the oven until they are quite tender, peel and slice them. Put them in a pan with a little butter, some finely chopped parsley and chives (or onion tops), a small clove of garlic, a pinch of flour and salt and pepper to taste. Add a very little vinegar and bring the mixture to the boil. Cook for about 15 minutes and serve very hot.

# Broccoli

This is a good all-the-year round vegetable and a good source of vitamins A, B and C. Both purple and white sprouting varieties are available.

# Broccoli and French Bean Salad

Cooked purple sprouting
    broccoli

1 large cup cooked French or
    runner beans

1 lettuce

1 bunch radishes

Mayonnaise (see page 174)

Chopped parsley

*A very good salad – you can use cauliflower if broccoli is not available – and you do not have to cook it, unless it is an old one.*

Line a bowl with lettuce leaves, and pile the broccoli in the centre. Toss the beans in the mayonnaise and arrange them around the broccoli. Halve the radishes, arrange them on top of the beans and sprinkle chopped parsley over the broccoli.

# Brussel Sprouts

One of the most easily obtainable vegetables, and usually very reasonably priced. Their protein content is medium, but they are high in vitamins, particularly vitamin C. They are almost invariably served as a boiled accompaniment to meat dishes, but they are also very good raw, in salads. You can make excellent soup from sprouts that have gone a bit limp and when chestnuts are cheap, try boiling some separately then mixing them with the cooked sprouts, a little butter and plenty of seasoning.

# Sprouts with Hollandaise Sauce

*A very good way of serving young fresh sprouts — they should be cooked very briefly. Take off any really coarse outside leaves, cut the sprouts in half and cook them in boiling salted water for about 5 minutes. Drain them and serve them with the following sauce:*

Put the vinegar, bay leaf and peppercorns into a small saucepan and boil until there is only about 1 tablespoon of the liquid left. Strain into a basin and allow it to cool. Using a double saucepan, or a basin in a pan of water, mix the egg yolks into the liquid with a wooden spoon. Stir gently so that the mixture is completely smooth. It is important that the mixture should not be allowed to boil at any point during the sauce-making. Cut the butter into very small pieces and add it to the warmed egg mixture bit by bit, very slowly. Stir all the time, and you should end up with a sauce of a mayonnaise-like consistency. When all the butter is added, add the lemon juice, and season to taste.

3 tablespoons wine vinegar
12 black peppercorns
2 egg yolks
4 oz. (120 g.) butter
1 bay leaf
Salt and pepper
A little lemon juice

# Cabbage

I think it is very well known now how good those hard white cabbages are when they are shredded and served raw in salad. They are almost invariably considerably cheaper than lettuce and are deliciously crunchy. All varieties of cabbage are said to have a high food value, and much can be made of the cabbage as a main course. The most important thing to remember when cooking cabbage as a simple boiled vegetable is that it requires very little cooking — about 5 minutes in boiling salted water is usually sufficient.

# Chinese Cabbage Hearts

*Again, if you grow your own vegetables, Chinese cabbage is well worth trying — you can sometimes buy it at the greengrocer, but it is often expensive. If you cannot get it, then use green or Savoy cabbage for this recipe, which will serve six.*

1 lb. (500 g.) Chinese, green or
    Savoy cabbage
3½ teaspoons cornflour
3 tablespoons milk
4 teaspoons chicken fat
Good pinch of salt
Pinch of sugar
¼ pint (150 ml.) chicken stock
A slice of ham

Slice the cabbage into strips and rinse them in cold water. Mix the cornflour and the milk until smooth. Heat the chicken fat in a heavy pan and add the cabbage. Stir it well, but do not let it brown. After 1 minute add the stock, salt and sugar, turn the heat right down, cover and simmer for no more than 10 minutes. The cabbage must remain crisp. Remove the cabbage to a serving dish and keep it hot. Add the cornflour mixture to the liquid in the pan and stir until it thickens; add more seasoning if necessary. Pour over the cabbage, and serve with the chopped ham sprinkled on top.

# The Cabbage of My House

*An excellent cabbage recipe which comes from a wartime book. It is a little bit fiddly — but tastes, and looks splendid. And it requires no accompaniments.*

1 large cabbage (Not one of the
hard white ones — you would
not be able to dismantle it)

A stuffing chosen from one of
the following, or your own
invention, as the name of
the recipe suggests:

1) Cooked rice

2) ½ thick lentil purée and ½ raw
grated carrots mixed
together

3) Cooked minced bacon, mixed
with raw rolled oats

4) Left-over vegetables, chopped
finely and mixed with minced
meat.

Carefully cut off the outer leaves of the cabbage, remove the hard stalks and scrub the leaves well, with plenty of cold water. Slice the stalks finely. Boil about ¼ pint (150 ml.) salted water in a large saucepan, add the sliced stalks and outer leaves, cover with a lid and boil for 1 minute. Turn the leaves over and boil for another minute. Remove the leaves carefully and leave to cool. Chop the cabbage heart, add it to the stalks in the pan, cover with the lid and boil for 1 minute. Remove from the heat and leave with the lid on for 10 minutes. Strain the leaves and stalks, reserving the liquid. Mix with your chosen stuffing. Grease a pudding basin that is roughly the same size as the original cabbage and arrange the outer leaves in the basin in much the same way as they were attached to the cabbage, keeping one or two aside. Pack the stuffing in and cover with the remaining leaves. Lay some bacon rind on top and cover with a pudding cloth tied firmly. Steam in boiling water for about 1½ hours. Turn out, keeping the whole intact, and serve with a gravy made from the stock, and flavoured as you like. The finished dish should look like a whole cabbage!

# Paprika Cabbage

*An Austrian cabbage dish, which will serve four.*

1 white cabbage
1 onion
1 green pepper (a large one)
3 oz. (90 g.) lard
Caraway seeds
Paprika
Salt and black pepper
½ pint (300 ml.) wine vinegar

Mix together the vinegar, salt and pepper, and about a teaspoon caraway seeds. Shred the cabbage and put it to marinate in the vinegar mixture for 12 hours. Slice and fry the onion in the melted lard, add the cabbage, sprinkle well with paprika and stew gently, with a cover on the pan, for about 1 hour, or until the cabbage is soft. Slice the green pepper very thinly and stir it, raw, into the cooked cabbage. Serve at once.

# Cabbage, Red

Red cabbage seems to be used very little except for pickling, but it is a very good vegetable with high food value.

# Apples with Red Cabbage

2 cooking apples
1 red cabbage
2 onions
2 oz. (60 g.) butter
2 eating apples
1 tablespoon brown sugar
1 tablespoon wine vinegar
Pinch ground cloves
Salt and freshly ground black pepper
Bay leaf

Shred the cabbage and cut out any really coarse stalks. Soak it in warm water for 1 hour. Fry the sliced onion in butter in a large pot, and when it begins to soften add the drained cabbage. Peel and slice all the apples and add them to the cabbage together with the sugar, the vinegar, cloves, bay leaf and seasoning. Cover and simmer very slowly for about 2 hours. Stir from time to time — and if you think it is getting too dry add a little water. Taste and adjust the seasoning, or add a little more sugar if necessary. This dish can be served cold but it is best hot.

# To Pickle Red Cabbage

*This recipe comes from the 1890 edition of the School Board for London's 'Cookery Book and General Axioms for Plain Cookery' formulated by Miss Briggs. I always use this method and it is very successful.*

Remove the outer leaves; quarter and cut out the thick stalk; with a sharp knife cut it thinly across into long strips. Reverse a plate in a large basin; on this put the shredded cabbage in layers, with a very light sprinkling of salt between each; cover with another plate, and on this put a weight to assist in pressing out the moisture. Let it remain thus for 24 hours; then squeeze it (without crushing it) in a thick cloth; and put it into jars or bottles. Boil the spices in ½ pint (300 ml.) vinegar for 15 minutes (an enamelled or preserving pan should be used); add the remainder of the vinegar, and pour it, when quite cold, on to the cabbage, enclosing the spices in a piece of muslin. Tie firmly over with thick paper, doubled, and it will be ready for use in about ten days or a fortnight.

And Miss Briggs adds the following note:
'When the vinegar is allowed to cool the pickles will become crisp; but anything green, such as gherkins or French beans, require the vinegar boiling when poured over, to keep the colour.'

1 cabbage
1 quart (1.2 litres) best vinegar
3 pieces whole ginger (sliced)
¼ oz. (10 g.) whole allspice
½ oz. (15 g.) whole pepper
    (black peppercorns)
12 cloves
Salt

# Carrots

Carrots are one of the most useful vegetables, and one of the most nourishing. When you clean them, remove as little of the red outer part as possible — it is the best part of the carrot. A good way of cooking them is to melt about ½ oz. (15 g.) butter in a saucepan, add the cleaned carrots, cut into small pieces, and stir them for about 5 minutes over gentle heat. Then add about ½ a cup of vegetable stock, cover tightly and cook them gently for about ½ an hour, shaking occasionally to prevent sticking or burning. Most of the liquid should be absorbed in the cooking. For the classic *carottes Vichy,* scrape some new carrots and cut them into rounds. Put them into a heavy pan with a lump of butter, a pinch of salt, 2 sugar lumps and ¾ pint (450 ml.) water for each lb. (500 g.) of carrots. Cook without a lid until almost all the liquid has evaporated and the carrots are tender. Add a little more butter, and shake the pan well. Serve with a little chopped parsley sprinkled over.

# Carrot Soufflé

Basic soufflé:

1 oz. (30 g.) cooking fat

1 oz. (30 g.) flour

3 eggs

¼ pint (150 ml.) milk

½ teaspoon yeast extract

2 cups cold cooked diced carrots

½ cup parsley or cheese sauce

*Carrots are used as the basis of a main dish in this wartime recipe.*

Grease a soufflé dish. Mix the carrots with the sauce and put them in the bottom of the dish. Melt the cooking fat in a pan, stir in the flour and cook very gently for a couple of minutes. Add the milk and bring to the boil. Remove from the heat, and mix in the well-beaten egg yolks and the yeast extract. Whisk the egg whites until stiff and mix them in lightly. Pour the mixture on top of the carrots, and bake in a hot oven (Gas mark 7, 425°F., 220°C.) for ½ hour. Serve at once. You may wish to tie a piece of greaseproof paper round the outside of the dish to steady the soufflé when it rises. Left-over leeks, spinach, or raw tomatoes are also very good in this soufflé.

# Carrot and Rice Pudding

*Another carrot main dish.*

1 lb. (500 g.) carrots, minced
½ pint (300 ml.) stock
2 oz. (60 g.) rice
¼ pint (150 ml.) milk
1 oz. (30 g.) butter
A heaped tablespoon breadcrumbs,
    mixed with grated cheese

Wash the carrots and mince them. Bring the stock to boil in a saucepan and add the carrots and the rice, season to taste, and simmer with a lid on for 30 minutes. Add the milk, reheat the mixture, and pour it into a greased fireproof dish. Sprinkle the top with the breadcrumbs and cheese, dot with butter and put under a hot grill to brown.

# Cauliflower

A very popular vegetable, with a high vitamin content, though not much protein. It can be cooked in a number of ways, eaten raw, if young enough, and it makes delicious soup. When serving it as a plain boiled vegetable be careful not to overcook it — it must never be soggy. If it is divided into individual sprigs then ten minutes in a little boiling salted water is sufficient. There are a number of ways ways in which cauliflower may be used to produce a main dish.

# Pain de Choufleur

*Cauliflower cake — enough for four people.*

Put the breadcrumbs and the milk into a pan, and stir them over heat until they boil and thicken. Add the butter and the cauliflower, in pieces, and mix well. Remove from the heat, and stir in the beaten egg yolks and seasoning to taste. Whip the egg whites until they are stiff, and mix them carefully into the

2 cups cooked cauliflower
1 cup breadcrumbs
1 cup milk
1 oz. (30 g.) butter
2 eggs
Salt and black pepper
2 tablespoons browned breadcrumbs

mixture. Grease a cake tin and coat it with the browned breadcrumbs, and pour in the cauliflower mixture. Stand the tin on a baking tin with a little hot water around it, and bake it in a moderate oven (Gas mark 5, Electric 375°F., 190°C) for about 30 minutes, until well-risen and firm to the touch. Turn it out on to a hot dish, and serve garnished with parsley.

# Cauliflower à l'Italienne

1 cooked cauliflower
½ pint (300 ml.) tomato sauce
   (see page 181)
2 tablespoons chopped mushrooms
2 tablespoons cooked tongue
1 tablespoon grated cheese
1 tablespoon breadcrumbs
A small piece of butter

*A way of using up left-over cooked tongue, and a very good and economical dish for four people.*

Break the cauliflower into sprigs (this can be done before it is cooked). Grease a fireproof dish and arrange in it, in layers, the cauliflower, the tomato sauce, the mushrooms and the chopped tongue. Mix the breadcrumbs and the cheese together and cover the top. Dot with butter and cook in a moderate oven (Gas mark 4, Electric 350°F., 180°C.) for 15 to 20 minutes until brown and crisp on top. Serve very hot.

# Cauliflower Suprème

1 cauliflower
¼ lb. (120 g.) peeled and thinly
   sliced mushrooms
2 oz. (60 g.) flour
Salt and Pepper
Top of the milk

Cook the cauliflower, reserving the water in which it is cooked, and sauté the mushrooms in butter for 10 minutes. Stir in flour, and salt and pepper to taste, and ½ pint (300 ml.) cauliflower water mixed with the top of the milk. Stir until this sauce is smooth and thick. Put the whole cauliflower into a serving dish and serve with the sauce poured over.

# Celeriac

Sometimes called turnip-rooted celery, this root vegetable tastes more or less the same as celery, and is sometimes available quite cheaply. It is very good peeled, grated and served raw as a salad; or it can be sliced after boiling and served as part of an hors d'oeuvre with a vinaigrette sauce. It also makes a good purée with a little butter, and some white sauce stirred in.

# Celery

A very useful vegetable which can be eaten raw or cooked. A valuable flavouring vegetable in stew and soups — use the green tops and the coarse outside stalks for this purpose. At one time it was claimed that celery had 'distinct medicinal value', and was recommended in the treatment of rheumatism — I cannot vouch for this, but certainly some of the late summer and autumn varieties are said to be of high food value. Stewed celery hearts, the old favourite method, is now too expensive, as you would have to allow one heart per person, but you can clean and chop a whole head of celery and then stew it gently in a mixture of butter and olive oil for about 15 minutes. Or you can stew it gently in oil, and serve it cold *( à la Grecque)* as an hors d'oeuvre.

# Celery au Gratin

*A popular way of serving many vegetables, such as cauliflower, leeks, marrow, onions or sprouts, during the post-war period of food rationing.*

Clean the celery and cut it into short lengths, using as much as possible, and keeping the rest for flavouring purposes, or putting it in your stock-pot. Heat 1 teaspoon of fat in a saucepan and cook the prepared celery for a few minutes, stirring constantly. Add 2 tablespoons of vegetable broth or stock, cover, and continue to cook gently, stirring now

1 head of celery

1 oz. (30 g.) cooking fat

1 tablespoon wholewheat flour

3 heaped tablespoons grated cheese

½ teaspoon yeast extract

¼ pint (150 ml.) milk

¼ pint (150 ml.) vegetable broth

and then to prevent burning. Melt the rest of the fat, stir in the flour, gradually add the milk and the remaining stock and allow to boil for 1 minute. Cool a little and stir in the yeast extract and all the cheese except for 1 dessertspoonful. When the celery is just tender, stir it into the cheese sauce, and pour the whole into a greased fireproof dish. Sprinkle with the rest of the cheese, and bake in a moderate oven (Gas mark 4, Electric 350°F., 180°C.) for about ½ hour.

# Courgettes

Usually considered to be a luxury vegetable, these small marrows are becoming increasingly popular among gardeners. They are easy to grow, and can be cooked in many ways. One of the simplest and best methods is simply to top, tail and slice them, and stew very gently in butter for about 10 minutes. Serve them sprinkled with salt and black pepper. Or slice 1½ lb. (750 g.) courgettes, sprinkle them with salt and leave them to drain in a colander for 1 hour – dry them and cook them gently in 3 oz. (90 g.) butter; when they begin to brown, stir in ¾ lb. (360 g.) peeled and chopped tomatoes, and cook over slightly higher heat until the tomatoes amalgamate with the butter to make a delicate sauce. Season with salt, pepper, and a little sugar to taste and serve hot with a sprinkling of chopped parsley.

# Cucumber

Cucumbers are invariably served as a salad vegetable, but they can also be cooked. You can peel them, cut them in half lengthways, and steam them, sprinkled with salt, pepper and a little lemon juice. Serve steamed cucumber with Hollandaise sauce (see page 122), and sprinkled with capers. Or make them into a main course according to the following recipe.

# Stuffed Cucumber

1 cucumber (per 2 persons)

1 cup cooked potato

2 tablespoons cooked ham

2 egg yolks

2 tablespoons grated cheese

2 tablespoons top of the milk

1 tablespoon breadcrumbs

A little butter

¼ pint (150 ml.) stock or white
    wine

Salt and black pepper

If possible get a short thick and fairly straight cucumber. Peel it thinly, and scald it in boiling water for about 10 minutes. Rinse it in cold water, cut it in half lengthways, and remove the seeds. Wrap it in a cloth while you prepare the stuffing. Put the potatoes through a sieve and add the finely chopped ham, the grated cheese and the seasoning. Mix well and stir in the egg yolks and enough milk to make a stiffish mixture. Put the cucumber in a long fireproof dish, and fill with the stuffing. Sprinkle with breadcrumbs, dot with butter and pour the stock or wine (or half and half) around. Bake in a moderate oven for 15—20 minutes (Gas mark 4, Electric 350°F., 180°C.) until the top is nicely browned.

# Dandelions

Not usually thought of as a vegetable, but available for everyone free of charge. Very young leaves can be served in salad, and larger leaves can be cooked like spinach — do not use very large leaves as they may be bitter. Dandelions have been said to be good for the liver. There is also a culinary dandelion which is very high in iron and other minerals, and has a lot of vitamin A. The leaves may be used for salad, the roots can be roasted, ground and used like coffee, and, last but not least, the flowers can be used for wine-making — a truly multi-purpose vegetable.

# Garlic

According to some of the ancient Greeks, and they were right about a lot of things, garlic is of great value medicinally; Nicholas Culpeper (1616—1654) said it is 'a remedy for all diseases and hurts'; and in some Mediterranean countries it is still believed to be a protection against the Evil Eye. It certainly figures largely in a number of modern herbal aids to health. But, aside from its medicinal properties, it is invaluable in the kitchen. It is quite easy to grow, as long as you water it during dry weather — mine failed last year because I neglected to do this. I have found that it is not advisable to buy garlic in large amounts as it tends to go powdery — better buy only a couple of bulbs at a time. How much you use in cooking is a matter of personal taste, but it is certainly true that a little crushed raw garlic is much more penetrating than a considerably larger quantity that has been cooked — it is also said that the more garlic you eat, the less you smell of it.

# Kale

A vegetable which seems to have gone out of fashion, although I remember having it often as a child. Clean it and chop it as for cabbage, cook it in boiling salted water for about 30 minutes. Drain the kale, squeeze it as dry as possible and chop it finely. Melt a little butter in a pan and add the chopped kale, shake it over the heat, seasoned with salt, pepper and a pinch of nutmeg. Heat thoroughly and serve. Turnip tops, if young and fresh, can be cooked in the same way.

# Kohl Rabi

Although a member of the cabbage family, this looks rather like a turnip. It is easy to grow, and is sometimes to be seen at the greengrocer. When young it can be eaten raw, or cooked in the same way as turnips, although it has a more delicate flavour. It is very good stewed with bacon.

# Leek

A very useful and justly popular vegetable, leeks are easy to grow, if you have the space, and are readily, and cheaply available from the greengrocer from September/October until April. According to an old cookery book, leeks are one of the 'healthiest of vegetables, particularly beneficial in cases of cold and chest trouble, and having a salutary effect on the liver.' Chop a little bacon and cook it in about 1 oz. (30 g.) butter, then add 1 lb. (500 g.) of cleaned leeks, and stew them gently for about 10–15 minutes with no extra water, and you have a delicious accompaniment to almost any dish. And don't throw away the green tops — either cook them as well, or use them for soup.

# Scottish Leek Pie

10 leeks
1 egg
2 cups milk
A little butter
Salt and pepper
Shortcrust pastry

Take the white part of the leeks, wash them well and cut them into small pieces. Boil them for 10 minutes, strain them and cook for a further 10 minutes in half the milk. Put them in a pie dish with a cup of milk into which you have beaten one egg. Season well with salt and plenty of black pepper. Add a few dots of butter, cover with shortcrust pastry and cook for ½ hour in a moderate oven (Gas mark 4, Electric 350ºF., 180ºC.) so that the pastry is nicely browned.

# Leek Tart

Shortcrust pastry
3 lb. (1.5 kg.) leeks
2 egg yolks beaten into ¼ pint
    (150 ml.) cream
Salt and pepper

*A delicious tart which can be served hot or cold.*

Line a tart tin with the pastry. Chop the white part of the leeks and melt them in about 2 oz. (60 g.) butter. Spread on the pastry and pour over the egg and cream mixture. Bake in a moderately hot oven for about 30 minutes (Gas mark 5, Electric 375ºF., 190ºC.). You can make this dish more substantial by cooking it on a bread dough, and by adding about 2 oz. (60 g.) chopped ham to the leeks.

# Marrow

A popular vegetable among gardeners, and available cheaply and plentifully during the summer months. They are best eaten young, and should not be allowed to get dry and hard after picking (or buying) and before cooking. Very young marrows can be eaten in the same ways as courgettes, and larger ones can be peeled, seeded, cooked in boiling salted water until tender and served with a cheese sauce — or the pieces can be roasted around meat. A very simple method of stuffing a marrow is to cut off a lid longways, scoop out the seeds, fill the cavity with sage and onion stuffing, replace the lid and tie with tape in two places. Bake in a moderate oven (Gas mark 3, Electric 325°F., 170°C.) for about 1½ hours — or 2 hours if it is a very large marrow. For a main course, make a stuffing with left-over cooked minced meat, tomatoes, breadcrumbs, minced onion and herbs, the whole being bound with an egg. In fact, you can stuff a marrow with almost anything you happen to have. It is very good in chutney (see page 180), and in Mexico the chopped flowers are used as the basis for a soup.

# Mushrooms

There are now several methods of growing mushrooms at home — in buckets and polythene sacks, but they are almost always available quite cheaply at the greengrocers. Mushroom stalks are sometimes sold separately, and these are very good for flavouring sauces and for making soup — they should be much cheaper than whole mushrooms. The small cultivated mushrooms should require little washing — just a quick rinse in cold water, and you do not need to peel them or remove the stalks.

# Stuffed Mushrooms

*A mushroom dish which could be served as a main course, accompanied by salad, or even green vegetables. Instead of the sausage meat you could use an 8 oz. (250 g.) tin of pressed pork or spiced beef. Try to use large mushrooms that are not too flat.*

6 large mushrooms

1 lb. (500 g.) sausage meat

2 oz. (60 g.) breadcrumbs

1 oz. (30 g.) suet

2 oz. (60 g.) butter

Salt and pepper

Parsley

Egg to bind

Skin the mushrooms and remove the stalks. Put them in a basin, pour some boiling water over, soak for 2 minutes, then drain. Form the sausage meat into six flat round cakes and put them in a baking tin with the mushrooms on top, the underside uppermost. Chop the mushroom stalks, and mix them with the breadcrumbs, suet, seasoning and parsley. Bind the mixture with a little egg and stuff the mushrooms. Put a little pat of butter on top of each and bake in a moderately hot oven (Gas mark 7, Electric 425°F., 220°C.) for ½ hour.

# Nasturtium

Both the flowers and the leaves of nasturtiums can be used raw in salads, and the young seeds can be pickled — they are a little like capers in flavour. The seeds should be gathered on a dry day and pickled in vinegar which has been boiled with 1 dessertspoon salt and 6 peppercorns per pint (per 600 ml.). Keep them at least two months before using.

# Nettles

The common stinging nettle contains iron and protein, and grows plentifully almost everywhere. Gather the young shoots (remember to wear gloves), wash them very thoroughly and remove any coarse stems. Use them to make nettle soup, which is really good (see p. 24) or cook them in the same way as spinach.

# Onions

A splendid vegetable, said to purify the blood and soothe the nerves, but certainly containing vitamins $B_1$, $B_2$, $B_6$, and C. Easy to grow, and able to be cooked in a number of different ways. Try baking them in a covered casserole with a little butter — large onions would take about 1½ hours in a moderate oven (Gas mark 4, Electric 350°F., 180°C.). When you slice them for frying, dip them in a little milk and then in seasoned flour first — not as soggy as ordinary fried onions.

# Stuffed Spanish Onions

*Make a main course out of those large Spanish onions that are so often in the shops. The following quantities are sufficient for four people.*

Skin the onions and boil them for 10 minutes in salted water, drain them and throw them into cold water. When cool enough to handle, remove two of the outer skins and carefully scoop out the centres making enough room for about 1 tablespoon of stuffing. Chop all these bits of onion and put them into a fireproof casserole with the butter and the stock, and keep them hot over a low heat. Chop the meat finely (you can use chicken, tongue, ham or anything you have) and put it into a basin with the breadcrumbs, parsley and the chopped mushrooms. Add enough tomato sauce to bind and season with salt, pepper and nutmeg. Fill the centres of the onions with this mixture, piling it quite high. Put them in the casserole with the chopped onion pieces and the stock, cover with greaseproof paper and then the lid. Bake in a moderate oven (Gas mark 3, Electric 325°F., 170°C.) for about 2 hours or until the onions are quite tender.

4 Spanish onions

2 tablespoons cooked meat (left-over)

2 tablespoons breadcrumbs

1 teaspoon chopped parsley

Salt and pepper

4 small mushrooms

Pinch nutmeg

1 tablespoon tomato sauce

1 oz. (30 g.) butter

¼ pint (150 ml.) stock

# Onion Crisp

12 small onions
½ pint (300 ml.) milk
4 tablespoons cooked peas
2½ oz. (75 g.) butter
2 oz. (60 g.) flour
Salt and pepper
2 oz. (60 g.) breadcrumbs
2 tablespoons minced salt
    peanuts

Peel the onions, boil them in milk and a little water until tender, then remove them whole and place in a greased fireproof dish with the peas. Make a thick sauce with the liquid in which the onions were cooked, 2 oz. (60 g.) of the butter and the flour. Season well — more pepper than salt. Pour over the onions, sprinkle with breadcrumbs and nuts, and put the rest of the butter on top in pieces. Brown under a very hot grill.

# Shallots

If you grow these yourself, you will find that the side shoots can be used as spring onions about six weeks after planting. Use them when larger for flavouring soups, stews, fish dishes or for pickling — they are ideal for this purpose, both in size and flavour.

# Parsnips

A very useful winter vegetable, delicious parboiled then fried in a little butter and served with a sprinkling of brown sugar. It is not generally known that the tops are also edible — the stems taste rather like celery, and the leaf can be used in salad. They are good roasted around meat, and make a delicious soufflé — use the recipe for artichoke soufflé (see page 117), but substitute a pinch of nutmeg for the lemon rind, and sprinkle with chopped nuts before cooking.

# Peas

Another good source of protein and vitamins — and remember you can use the pods for soup (see page 26).

# Green Peas with Lettuce

1 pint (600 ml.) shelled peas
1 young lettuce
2 spring onions
A good sprig parsley
Salt and white pepper
½ teaspoon sugar
1½ oz. (45 g.) butter
½ oz. (15 g.) flour

Put the peas into a saucepan with the shredded lettuce, the onions and 1 oz. (30 g.) butter. Pour over enough boiling water to barely cover and cook slowly until the peas are tender (10–15 minutes). Lift out the onions and the parsley, and mix the flour smoothly with the ½ oz. (15 g.) butter and stir this into the peas. Cook for a few more minutes and serve very hot.

# Fresh Green Pea Soufflé

*A delightful summer dish.*

½ pint (300 ml.) shelled young
   peas
2 eggs
¼ teaspoon salt
½ pint (300 ml.) water
1 oz. (30 g.) butter
Sprig of mint

Boil the peas in the water with ½ oz. (15 g.) butter, mint and salt for ½ hour uncovered. When ready, take out the mint and stand the saucepan on one side to cool a little. Well grease a soufflé dish with the rest of the butter. Beat the egg yolks and stir them into the cooled peas. Whisk the whites stiffly and fold them into the mixture. Pour into the soufflé dish and bake for about 20 minutes in a hot oven (Gas mark 7, Electric 425°F., 220°C.).

# Peppers

I have grown peppers successfully on a sunny window sill. They can be used in a variety of ways, including raw in salads. A substantial meal can be made by stuffing them with a mixture of cooked rice, chopped tomatoes, left-over cooked meat and herbs – put them in a casserole with a little dilute tomato sauce and cook them in a moderate oven for about 30 minutes (Gas mark 6, Electric 400°F., 200°C.).

# Potatoes

It would be possible to devote a whole chapter to potatoes, there are so many things you can do with them, but space does not permit it. So I have chosen one or two recipes which make full use of this vegetable as a main course. If you are baking potatoes in their jackets, remember to rub them well with salt before you cook them — the skins then taste delicious. If you have boiled potatoes left over, slice them, mix in a little crushed garlic and sauté them in a little oil. Left-over mashed potato can be mixed well with grated cheese, beaten egg yolks, salt, pepper and a little made mustard — put the whole in a greased fireproof dish, sprinkle with breadcrumbs and a few dots of butter and brown under a hot grill.

# Potato and Cheese Mould

½ lb. (250 g.) cooked potatoes
2 oz. (60 g.) grated cheese
2 tablespoons milk
2 eggs
Salt and pepper
Browned breadcrumbs

Sieve the potatoes and add the melted butter, the egg yolks, cheese, seasoning and the milk. Mix well together. Whisk the egg whites stiffly and stir them lightly into the mixture. Grease a pudding basin and line it with the browned breadcrumbs. Three-parts fill with the mixture and bake in a moderate oven (Gas mark 4, Electric 350°F. 180°C.) for about ½ hour. Turn out on to a hot serving dish and serve at once, garnished with sprigs of parsley.

# Stuffed Potatoes

Choose potatoes of equal size and scrub them well, then bake them for about 1 hour in a hot oven (Gas mark 7, Electric 425°F., 220°C.). Cut a small piece off the end of each potato and scoop out the flesh with a teaspoon, being careful not to damage the skin. Mash this flesh in a basin, and add to it the finely chopped meat (or fish, or grated cheese), the

4 or 6 potatoes
3 or 4 tablespoons cooked meat
1 teaspoon chopped parsley
2 tablespoons top of the milk
Salt and pepper
A little butter
Breadcrumbs

seasoning and the parsley. Mix well and bind with the milk. Fill the potatoes with this mixture, press it well down, and put the little lids back on. If the stuffing protrudes, do not put the lids on — instead sprinkle the top of the stuffing with breadcrumbs and put a little pat of butter on top. Stand the potatoes upright in the dish and return to the oven to heat thoroughly (about ½ hour).

# To Cook New Potatoes Perfectly

*New potatoes are so delicious that it is worth going to a bit of trouble when cooking them — this method, en papillotes, or in a paper bag, seems to work everytime, and is especially good for those very small potatoes at the beginning of the season.*

Wash and dry about 2 dozen very small new potatoes — there is no need to scrape them unless you really want to. Have ready a fairly large piece of grease-proof paper and put the potatoes on it with 2 mint leaves, 2 oz. (60 g.) butter, and sprinkle with a little salt. Fold the paper over and fold the edges so that the bag is completely sealed. Preheat the oven to Gas mark 5, Electric 375°F., 190°C., and cook the potatoes for about 35 minutes

# Sorrel

Sorrel is not a widely used vegetable, but it is very easy to grow in the garden, or in large pots, and it will come up year after year. It can be cooked like spinach, but it cooks more rapidly. It is very good in soup, and makes a delicious filling for an omelette. Make a purée of sorrel, flavoured with a little French tarragon mustard, mix in two egg yolks, and serve as a bed for poached fish.

141

# Spinach

A vegetable that is very high in calcium, protein, iron and vitamins A and C. It is easy to grow, and usually easily obtainable from the greengrocer throughout the year, there being summer and winter varieties. It must be washed very thoroughly, and any discoloured leaves should be removed — allow about ½ lb. (250 g.) per person. Never add water when you cook spinach — it will cook in the water it retains from the washing process, and remember that it cooks quickly, so keep an eye on it, and stir it with a wooden spoon from time to time. After about 10 minutes, turn it into a colander, put a plate on top, and then a weight and leave it for about 5 minutes. Chop it and heat it for a few minutes in melted butter.

# Spinach Soufflé

*A very good soufflé, for which it is worth trying to use cream if you can. The quantities given here would provide a light lunch dish for two, or an hors d'oeuvre for four.*

1 lb. (500 g.) spinach
2 tablespoons cream or white sauce
Salt and pepper
2 eggs
1 tablespoon browned breadcrumbs
A little grated cheese (optional)
Lemon juice
Nutmeg

Prepare and cook the spinach as described above, but do not cook in butter. Drain the spinach well and rub it through a sieve, put the purée in a basin, add pepper, salt, a squeeze of lemon juice, and a pinch of nutmeg. Add the egg yolks and cheese, if you wish, and mix well. If you are using cream, whip it and then add it to the mixture. Beat the egg whites stiffly and stir them lightly into the mixture. Pour the mixture into a well-greased soufflé dish, sprinkle the top with browned breadcrumbs and bake in a moderate oven for 20–30 minutes until well risen and firm to the touch. (Gas mark 4, Electric 350°F., 180°C.).

# Spinach and Cheese Tart

Shortcrust pastry case cooked 'blind'

1 lb. (500 g.) spinach

2 oz. (60 g.) butter or margarine

4 oz. (120 g.) grated cheese

Pinch of pepper

Cook the spinach in the usual way. Drain it well and chop it. Return to the pan with half the butter and cook it quickly until fairly dry. Add three-quarters of the cheese and mix well. Pile this mixture into the pastry case and sprinkle with the rest of the grated cheese. Melt the remaining butter and pour it over. Cook in a hot oven (Gas mark 7, Electric 425°F., 220°C.) until the cheese has melted and is nicely brown (about 15 minutes).

# Swede

Swedes should be well scrubbed, peeled fairly thickly, then cut into smallish pieces. Cook in boiling salted water until tender (½–1 hour according to size and age). Drain them well, then mash them with butter, and a sprinkling of salt and plenty of black pepper. Serve with a sprinkling of chopped parsley.

# Sweetcorn

This is becoming popular with gardeners, but it does take up a lot of room. It can be expensive to buy fresh, but it is quite delicious boiled on the cob in salted water for about 20 minutes and served with melting butter. And it is high in protein. The tinned varieties are also useful.

# Tuna Corn Bake

¾ pint (450 ml.) white sauce

2 oz. (60 g.) chopped mushrooms

2  7 oz. (200 g.) tins tuna

12 oz. (360 g.) tin of sweetcorn

*Very quick and economical.*

Mix everything together thoroughly, and put in a greased fireproof dish (sprinkle with a mixture of breadcrumbs and grated cheese, if you wish). Bake in a hot oven (Gas mark 7, Electric 425°F., 220°C.) for about 15 minutes, and then brown under a hot grill. Serve garnished with sliced green pepper, and triangles of toast.

143

# Tomatoes

If you haven't a garden, or a greenhouse, try growing tomatoes on your windowsill — there are some new varieties available which will produce heavy crops. If you can't grow your own, and are buying tomatoes for cooking, be sure to tell the greengrocer this — he invariably has some over-ripe ones which he will sell more cheaply than the choice salad varieties.

# Tomato Pudding

2 oz. (60 g.) mushrooms
1 oz. (30 g.) butter
1 chopped onion
1 lb. (500 g.) tomatoes
4 oz. (120 g.) white breadcrumbs
Salt and pepper
1 egg
½ pint (300 ml.) stock
Baked halved tomatoes for
    garnish

Peel, wash and slice the mushrooms (unless they are very small ones, in which case don't peel them). Melt the butter and fry the sliced mushrooms with the chopped onion. Slice the tomatoes. Put alternate layers of tomatoes, mushroom mixture, and breadcrumbs in a fireproof dish, seasoning each layer with salt and pepper. Beat the egg into the stock and pour over the vegetables. Bake in a moderate oven (Gas mark 4, Electric 350°F., 180°C.) for 45 minutes and serve garnished with baked tomatoes.

# Tomatoes and Lentils

2 oz. (60 g.) red lentils
1 onion
2 tomatoes
1 teaspoon tomato purée
A pinch salt
½ pint (300 ml.) water
1 egg

*A very tasty and nutritious soufflé. Use red lentils.*

Chop the onion and put it with the lentils and water into a small pan. Cook until soft. Skin the tomatoes, press through a sieve, and stir into the mixture in the pan. Allow to cool, then add the beaten egg yolk. Beat the white stiffly and fold it into the mixture. Pour into a well-greased soufflé dish, and bake for about 30 minutes (Gas mark 4, Electric 350°F., 180°C.).

# Turnips

There is often confusion about what is a turnip and what is a swede — the answer is that they are both turnips! What we call a swede is in fact a turnip with orange flesh, and what we call a turnip is a white turnip. Very small white turnips are lovely if they are roasted whole, or boiled and served with a parsley sauce. Unless the turnips are young, they are best puréed, with butter, in the same way as swede (see page 143).

# Turnips with Ham

2 lb. (1 kg.) very small turnips
1½ oz. (45 g.) butter
4 oz. (120 g.) ham, cut into
    strips

Skin the turnips very thinly and cook them in boiling salted water for ten minutes. Drain, halve them, and gently saute them in the melted butter for about 15 minutes with the pan covered. Shake the pan now and then to make sure the turnips do not stick. Then stir in the ham, heat through, and serve with a good sprinkling of chopped chives on top.

# Pulses

Now that meat is a very expensive item, it is as well to look for other sources of protein and pulses — lentils, butter beans, haricot beans, split peas — are a cheap and valuable source. The protein constituent of lentils is said to be around 23%, whereas that of medium fat meat is around 20%. Many delicious meals can be prepared with pulses, and such dishes are frequently popular with children — every child seems to be devoted to tinned baked beans, which are basically haricot beans in tomato sauce. Another great advantage is that pulses can be kept for months in the store cupboard — but remember that they will not keep forever, as you will quickly discover if you try to cook haricots that have been around for about two years! All dried pulses must be soaked before cooking, except lentils — but don't add salt to the water in which you soak them as this tends to harden them.

# Boston Baked Beans

*Really delicious — you can use pickled pork if you are able to get it, but I invariably use belly pork, or fat bacon. It takes ages to cook, but at a very low temperature.*

1 lb. (500 g.) haricot beans
8 oz. (250 g.) pork or bacon
    (see above)
2 oz. (60 g.) brown sugar
1 tablespoon black treacle
½ teaspoon made mustard
Salt

Soak the beans for 12 hours, or overnight, in plenty of cold water. Drain them, and cover them with fresh water and simmer until the skins are soft — they should burst if you blow on them. Cut a thick slice from the pork or bacon and put it into the bottom of a casserole. Remove the rind from the rest of the meat and cut it into pieces. Put the beans into the casserole and mix in the pieces of meat, the sugar, treacle, mustard and salt. Cover with boiling water or stock, and cook in the oven (covered) for 8 hours (Gas mark ¼, Electric 225°F., 110°C.). Check from time to time to see if more water is needed.

# Onion, Tomato and Haricot Pie

*Another wartime recommended dish — described as an 'appetising meal without using the meat ration'. A nutritious and filling meal.*

1 lb. (500 g.) onions
2 oz. (60 g.) flour
½ pint (300 ml.) milk
½ pint (300 ml.) onion water
2·oz. (60 g.) grated cheese
2 teaspoons salt
½ teaspoon pepper
¼ teaspoon dry mustard
8 oz. (250 g.) tomatoes (tinned
    or bottled)
8 oz. (250 g.) haricot beans

Wash the beans and soak them overnight. Drain them and boil in fresh water until they are tender, then rinse and drain. Peel and slice the onions and boil them in water until tender; strain and save the liquor. Blend the flour with the milk and onion water, stir it until it boils and boil for three minutes. Add the grated cheese and seasoning to this sauce and continue to cook very gently until the cheese has melted, stirring all the time. Grease a pie dish and arrange the onions, tomatoes and beans in layers, cover with the sauce and bake for about 20 minutes in a hot oven (Gas mark 7, Electric 425°F., 220°C.).

# Haricot Bean Casserole

*If you can't get Jerusalem artichokes, substitute some other root vegetable. This is a very good nourishing stew particularly recommended during the last war, as it contains no meat, but provides plenty of protein.*

4 oz. (120 g.) haricot beans
½ an onion
½ small head celery
2 tomatoes
3 artichokes
Salt and pepper
Bunch fresh herbs
1 pint (600 ml.) stock or water
A little milk
1 oz. (30 g.) fat
1 oz. (30 g.) flour
Grated cheese

Wash the beans and soak them overnight in plenty of cold water. Drain and cook in boiling salted water until tender, then rinse and drain. Place in a greased casserole. Chop the onion finely. Wash the celery, peel the tomatoes and artichokes and cut all into small pieces. Put all the vegetables into the casserole and season well. Add the bunch of herbs (if you have to use dried herbs, tie them in a piece of muslin), and pour in the stock or water. Cover with a tightly fitting lid and cook in a slow oven (Gas mark 2, Electric 300°F., 150°C.) for about 2½ hours. Drain off the liquid and make it up to 1 pint (600 ml.) with milk. Melt the fat and stir in the flour. Season well. Stir in the bean liquid and milk mixture, bring to the boil and cook for a few minutes, stirring all the time. Pour this sauce over the vegetables in the casserole, sprinkle with grated cheese, brown under a hot grill and serve.

# Butter Beans with Lemon

*The ideal lemon flavouring for this dish would be lemon balm which you may have in your garden, or perhaps would get from a friend. Otherwise, use lemon juice, but not too much as the lemon must not overwhelm the delicate flavour of the beans.*

1 pint (600 ml.) butter beans
1 oz. (30 g.) butter
1 tablespoon minced parsley
1 tablespoon finely-minced balm

Soak the beans for 12 hours or overnight in plenty of cold water. Drain, and cook gently in fresh water until tender (about 1½ – 2 hours). Melt the butter in a pan, and add the drained cooked beans. Toss them well, and, just before serving, stir in the parsley and balm.

# Butter Beans in Sauce

*Originally a Mexican dish, this is a splendid way of cooking butter beans (also called Lima beans). For years I was put off butter beans by the dreary things we were served at school — constantly being told that they were good for us. But fortunately I discovered that because something was good for one, it didn't have to be dull and nasty. So if you have similar memories, try this:*

1 lb. (500 g.) butter beans
4 oz. (120 g.) bacon
1 sliced onion
1 lb. (500 g.) tomatoes
1 tablespoon black treacle
1 tablespoon chilli powder
1 teaspoon salt

Soak the beans for 12 hours in plenty of cold water, drain and put into a casserole. Slice the bacon and mix it in. Cover with sliced onion and tomato, and sprinkle with chilli powder and salt. Dissolve the treacle in ½ pint (300 ml.) warm water, and pour over the beans. Cover and cook in a slow oven (Gas mark 2, Electric 300°F., 150°C.) for 2 hours.
N.B. The quantity of chilli powder given makes a very hot dish — I recommend 1 *teaspoon* the first time you cook this!

# Lentils

The most common, and cheapest lentils are the red ones (also called Egyptian lentils). These do not require any soaking, although I often cover them with cold water, and pick out any odd brown or black ones that float to the top. They are a very good addition to soups and stews, especially when you want to use little or no meat. The larger brown (greeny-brown) lentils are better for other types of dish, such as lentils and bacon (see page 80). Lentils are often thought of as filling winter vegetables, but you can make a very good salad with them too.

# Simple Lentil Roast

*A very popular vegetarian dish — the original recipe calls for nut fat, but you can use butter instead. I do recommend that you use wholemeal breadcrumbs, however — they give a much better flavour than white ones.*

½ lb. (250 g.) red lentils
½ pint (300 ml.) cold water
12 oz. (360 g.) grated raw turnip
4 oz. (120 g.) wholemeal bread-
    crumbs
1 egg
2 oz. (60 g.) butter
3 level tablespoons chopped ~~mint~~
    fresh mint

Cook the lentils in the water until they are soft and all the water has been absorbed. Add the butter and the mint, mix in thoroughly and then add the turnip and the breadcrumbs. Stir thoroughly and bind with the beaten egg. The mixture will be fairly moist because of the turnips. Put into a greased pie dish and bake in a fairly hot oven (Gas mark 6, Electric 400°F., 200°C.) for 30 minutes. Alternatively, form the mixture into rissoles, roll them in oatmeal and fry until they are brown all over.

# Lentils with Sausages

*This is a substantial dish for about four people — it is a favourite with children. Use whatever sausages you like, but beef ones seem to go particularly well.*

2 lb. (1 kg.) sausages
2 tablespoons red lentils
2 medium onions
1 clove garlic
1 bayleaf
2 cloves
½ teaspoon black peppercorns
Salt
Plain flour

Roll the sausages in plain flour. Slice the onions and garlic thinly. Put the sausages, onions and lentils in a fireproof casserole in layers. Add the spices and the bayleaf, cover with water and bake, with the lid on, in a slow oven for about 2½ hours. (Gas mark 1, Electric 275°F., 140°C.).

# Lentil Salad

8 oz. (250 g.) brown lentils
1 medium onion, sliced
Olive oil
Hard-boiled egg

Soak the lentils for a couple of hours in cold water, and pick out any bits that float to the surface. Cover with fresh water and cook for 1½ hours. Strain them and stir in very thinly sliced onion and plenty of olive oil. Season to taste and leave to get cold. Serve garnished with hard-boiled egg.

# Chick Peas

Unfortunately chick peas are rather difficult to get outside of the larger towns and cities. They are very good, but they need lengthy soaking and cooking. Soak them for 24 hours and put them in a large thick pan well-covered with water. Add a sliced onion, salt, pepper, two sage leaves, and two cloves of garlic. Cook them on the lowest possible heat until tender (2 − 6 hours) − do not be tempted to stir them, and do not let them stop boiling during this time, or they will never get soft. You may be able to get tinned chick peas − in which case, deal with them as directed.

# Hummus Bi Tahina

*Often called simply Hummus (which means chick peas), this is a very popular hors d'oeuvre which is Arab in origin. Tahina is a sesame paste which is obtainable in larger towns. It is fairly expensive but it keeps well, so buy it when you see it and put it in your store cupboard. There are variations on the recipe, some tending to be extravagant in the quantity of oil used, but the following version is the most economical I have tried.*

Soak the chick peas and boil them in fresh water until they are soft. Drain them and put aside a few whole ones to use as a garnish. Reduce the chick peas to a purée either by sieving, pounding in a mortar, or in an electric blender. If you use a blender add the lemon juice and a little water at the same time as the peas and when you have a purée add the garlic, salt and tahina and continue blending until you have a creamy paste.

If you are blending by hand, crush the garlic with some salt and pound it into the crushed peas until well mixed. Then add the tahina and lemon juice gradually, beating thoroughly. You may need to add a little water to get a nice creamy texture. Taste and add more lemon juice, salt or garlic if necessary. Pour the paste into a shallow dish. Mix the olive oil and paprika together and pour it carefully over the surface of the paste. Before serving sprinkle the parsley or mint over, and decorate with the whole chick peas.

4 oz. (120 g.) chick peas
Juice of 2 lemons
2 cloves garlic
Salt
¼ pint (150 ml.) tahina
1 tablespoon olive oil
1 teaspoon paprika
1 tablespoon chopped parsley
    or mint

# Chick Pea Balls

*A very good starter, or, if made in the quantities given below, good for a party dish. Cook the chick peas as described above.*

1 lb. (500 g.) chick peas
3 slices white bread, without crusts
2 eggs
Garlic
¼ teaspoon chilli powder
1 teaspoon salt
Black pepper

Mince or grind the cooked peas with the bread. Stir in the beaten eggs, the crushed garlic (use as little or as much as you like), the chilli powder and the salt and pepper. Mix everything together thoroughly and then form into balls or sausage-shapes with floured hands. Stand these in the fridge for an hour or two, then fry in hot fat until nicely browned all over. Serve with mustard, or some very piquant sauce.

# Chick Pea Salad

8 oz. (250 g.) chick peas
2 tablespoons olive oil
1 teaspoon vinegar
1 teaspoon French mustard
Garlic
Salt and pepper
Finely chopped onion and/or
green pepper (optional)

Cook the chick peas as instructed (p. 150). Drain and while still warm stir in the dressing made by mixing the olive oil, vinegar, French mustard, crushed garlic well together and seasoned to taste. Leave to cool and before serving add the onion and green pepper.
*Note:* Plain cooked chick peas make a delicious accompaniment to roast meat (especially lamb) if the meat juices are stirred into the peas while hot. Serve immediately. They can also be minced with a little cooked rice, cold meat, onion and seasoning to make an unusual filling for stuffed tomatoes, peppers, courgettes and so on.

# Chick Peas with Calf's Feet

2 calf's feet (or trotters)
Oil for frying
8 oz. (250 g.) chick peas
Salt and pepper
Crushed garlic
1 teaspoon paprika
Pinch of cayenne
1 large onion
4 tomatoes skinned and chopped

*Pig's trotters can be substituted for the calf's feet in this dish — a sort of Middle Eastern cassoulet.*

Soak the chick peas overnight. Wash the calf's feet; scrape and split them. Put them into a pan of cold water and bring to the boil. Remove from heat and throw away water together with any scum which may have accumulated. Rinse and dry feet and fry them in a heavy pan or casserole for a few minutes in a little oil until lightly browned. Add sliced onion, garlic, salt and pepper, cayenne, paprika and the drained chick peas. Cover with water and simmer gently for about 3 hours until meat is tender. Add tomatoes ¾ hour before end of cooking time.

# Dried Green Peas

If you want to use dried green peas as a substitute for the fresh ones, try to get the ones called marrow fat peas. If you are going to put them into a stew or casserole do remember that they will have to be soaked and that the dish to which they are being added must be one that is going to be cooked for 2 or 3 hours, or they will remain hard.

# To Cook Dried Green Peas

*This is a recipe which I found in a Victorian book where pulses were much recommended: '. . . very valuable articles of food on account of their low price and the amount of nourishment they contain. . .' Cooked according to this method, dried green peas make a very good winter vegetable, and, if you wish, you can purée them, or even thin down the purée with milk, or water, and serve them as soup.*

½ pint (300 ml.) dried green peas
1 onion
Salt and pepper
3 or 4 cloves
A bunch of herbs
2 tablespoons stock or cream
1 oz. (30 g.) butter
½ teaspoon sugar

Soak the peas for 12 to 18 hours in plenty of cold water, drain them and rinse them in fresh cold water. Put them in a saucepan covered with cold water and bring them slowly to the boil. Add the onion stuck with cloves and the herbs (if dried ones, tie them in muslin), and cook slowly for about 2½ hours until the peas are quite tender. If the peas become too dry during the cooking, add more water. Drain them when tender, and remove the onion and herbs. Return the peas to the pan, stir in the butter and the stock or cream. Season to taste and serve at once.

# Split Peas

Split peas can be used in most of the same ways as lentils, and must always be soaked overnight before cooking. In Sweden a very sustaining split pea soup is eaten prior to the Good Friday fast. 1 lb. (500 g.) peas are cooked in the water in which they were soaked, and the skins are skimmed off as they rise to the surface — then ½ lb. (250 g.) pork is added and the whole simmered for about 2 hours. The pork is removed and the soup sieved and seasoned with salt, pepper and ½ teaspoon ground ginger. The pork is then served as a side dish, with mustard. And then there is good old English Pease Pudding:

# Pease Pudding

½ lb. (250 g.) split peas
1 oz. (30 g.) butter
1 egg
Salt, pepper and a pinch of sugar

Wash the peas well and soak them overnight in plenty of cold water. Tie them loosely in a cloth (they will swell) and put them into a pan with a pinch of salt and enough boiling water to cover. Boil quickly for about 2 – 2½ hours, or until the peas are quite soft. Make sure they are well-covered with water all the time. Drain them and rub them through a colander. Add the butter, the well-beaten egg, salt, pepper and sugar and mix together very thoroughly. Flour another pudding cloth and tie the pea mixture up tightly this time. Boil for another ½ hour, and serve as an accompaniment to salt beef, boiled bacon, or tongue.

# Sweets

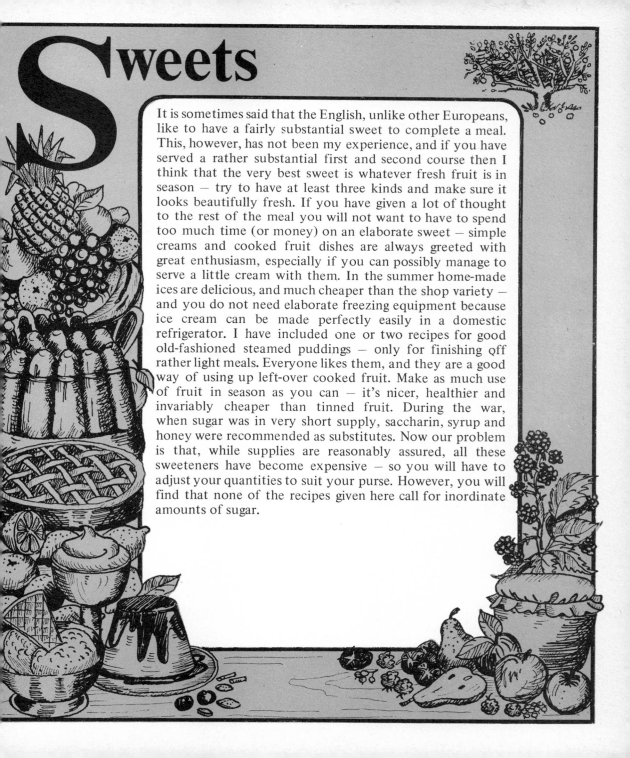

It is sometimes said that the English, unlike other Europeans, like to have a fairly substantial sweet to complete a meal. This, however, has not been my experience, and if you have served a rather substantial first and second course then I think that the very best sweet is whatever fresh fruit is in season — try to have at least three kinds and make sure it looks beautifully fresh. If you have given a lot of thought to the rest of the meal you will not want to have to spend too much time (or money) on an elaborate sweet — simple creams and cooked fruit dishes are always greeted with great enthusiasm, especially if you can possibly manage to serve a little cream with them. In the summer home-made ices are delicious, and much cheaper than the shop variety — and you do not need elaborate freezing equipment because ice cream can be made perfectly easily in a domestic refrigerator. I have included one or two recipes for good old-fashioned steamed puddings — only for finishing off rather light meals. Everyone likes them, and they are a good way of using up left-over cooked fruit. Make as much use of fruit in season as you can — it's nicer, healthier and invariably cheaper than tinned fruit. During the war, when sugar was in very short supply, saccharin, syrup and honey were recommended as substitutes. Now our problem is that, while supplies are reasonably assured, all these sweeteners have become expensive — so you will have to adjust your quantities to suit your purse. However, you will find that none of the recipes given here call for inordinate amounts of sugar.

# Stewed Rhubarb (Sugar Saving) and Whipped Cream

*Two interesting wartime recipes which come from a book specially designed for young and inexperienced cooks — they are a good example of the ways in which people really had to be ingenious and make the best of what was available — and they are nice.*

Cut 1 lb. (500 g.) rhubarb into 1 in. pieces (or you can use green gooseberries or sour plums). Put them into a saucepan with 1/8 pint (75 ml.) water and bring to the boil. Now add ½ level teaspoon bicarbonate of soda and simmer gently for 5 minutes. When it stops frothing add sugar to taste and simmer till tender. You use far less sugar this way.

For the whipped cream:
Dissolve ½ level tablespoon gelatine and ½ level tablespoon sugar in 3 tablespoons hot water until no grains remain — don't let it boil. Pour ½ tin evaporated milk into a bowl and add the cooled gelatine mixture. Beat with a whisk or a fork until the mixture is thick and fluffy (about ten minutes). Use the cream at once if it is to top stewed fruit. The longer it is left to stand the thicker it gets.

# Apple Whip

*Serve this whip in separate little dishes — not only does this look attractive, but it also gives you control over quantities.*

½ pint (300 ml.) apple purée
2 egg whites
2 tablespoons cream

Stew some good juicy apples to a thick pulp, sweeten them to taste and flavour with a little lemon juice. Beat the pulp until it is completely smooth (you can sieve it if you like). Whisk the egg whites until they are very stiff, add them to the purée and whisk both together until it is light and frothy. Whip the cream, and stir it in just before serving.

# Summer Pudding

*A recipe to be found in many cookery books — I have found a version which specifies rhubarb and is called Dr. Johnson's Pudding. Miss Briggs, in her 'Cookery Book and General Axioms for Plain Cooking' calls it a 'very cheap wholesome pudding', which it certainly is — but she does not say how delicious it is. Use whatever stewed fruit you have, and serve it with cream or ice cream.*

Line a pudding basin with slices of bread (white or brown, with the crusts removed). Pour in hot stewed fruit — a mixture of fruit is very good — and cover with a lid of bread. Put a saucer on top and a weight and leave until the next day. Turn out — the fruit should be completely sealed inside, and the juice should have soaked into the bread, making it an attractive colour.

# Gooseberry Fool

*A traditional English dish, which can be frozen and thus turned into Gooseberry Ice Cream — put it in the ice tray with foil over it and freeze for about 2½ hours — but be sure to stir it at least twice while it is freezing. If you are lucky enough to find wild gooseberries these are perfect for Fool, as they are hard and sharp. There is no need to top and tail the fruit, because all the bits come out in the sieving process.*

1 lb. (500 g.) hard green
    gooseberries
¼ lb. (120 g.) sugar
¼ pint (150 ml.) thick cream —
    during the war people some-
    times substituted custard, but
    cream really is much better.

Steam the gooseberries with the sugar until they are quite soft. Sieve them and let this purée get quite cold. Stir in the cream and serve the Fool very cold.

# Kick Pudding

1 lemon
1 apple
1 egg
1 oz. (30 g.) butter
2 oz. (60 g.) sugar
Shortcrust pastry

# Orange and Lemon Mould

1 lemon
1 orange
1 pint (600 ml.) water
2 tablespoons sugar
½ oz. (15 g.) butter
2 oz. (60 g.) cornflour
1 egg

# Urny Pudding

2 eggs
Their weight in flour and butter
The weight of 1 egg in sugar
½ teaspoon bicarbonate of soda
2 tablespoons strawberry jam

*A good sweet to serve hot or cold the sharpness of the lemon gives it its name.*

Line a greased sandwich tin with the pastry, and make the filling as follows:
Cream the butter and the sugar together. Add the well-beaten egg, the grated rind and juice of the lemon and the apple, which you have peeled, cored and cut into very small pieces. Mix well together and leave to stand for about ½ hour.
Pour into the pastry and bake in a moderate oven (Gas mark 4, Electric 350°F., 180°C.) for ½ hour, or until golden brown.

Peel the rind from the lemon and orange as thinly as possible. Put it into a pan with the water, and let it simmer slowly to extract the flavour. Mix the cornflour with a little cold water, and then strain the water from the rind on to it, stirring all the time. Return to the saucepan and stir over the heat until boiling — cook for about 10 minutes. Remove the pan from the heat and stir in the sugar, the butter, the strained juice of the fruit, and the well beaten egg. Mix together thoroughly and pour into a wet mould. Leave in a cool place and allow to set. Turn out and serve.

*As far as I know, this steamed pudding is Scottish in origin — it is very good, just like the puddings I remember as a child.*

Cream the butter and sugar, beating them to a cream, and gradually add the flour and the beaten eggs. Stir in the jam and the soda. Grease a pudding basin and half-fill it with the mixture, cover securely with greased paper and a pudding cloth and steam for 1½ hours.

# Compôte of Bananas

*A delicious sweet — if you have a little white wine, use that instead of the water — and you can use a lemon instead of the orange. In the old days, good cooks were always instructed to slice bananas with a silver knife, so that they would not discolour — but they discolour when cooked anyway.*

3 large bananas
2 oz. (60 g.) sugar
Rind and juice of 1 orange
2 tablespoons chopped walnuts
A little water (or wine)

Peel the bananas and cut them into pieces about 1 in. thick. Put them in a fireproof dish with the grated rind and juice of the orange, the sugar and the nuts. Add only enough water or wine to stop the bananas sticking, cover with a lid, and leave to simmer until the bananas are soft, but not broken. Serve warm.

# Caramel Custard

*A very simple and foolproof method of cooking this universally popular sweet; serve it hot if you like — I prefer it cold.*

Boil together 1 large tablespoon sugar and 2 table-spoons water until it is coffee-coloured — be very careful not to let it burn. Pour it into a bowl and turn about until the bowl is coated.
Make a custard with 2 eggs and a dessertspoon of sugar beaten well together; stir into 2 small teacups warm milk and pour into the prepared bowl. Cover with greased paper and steam gently for about 45 minutes by standing the bowl in a roasting tin with a little water and putting it in a slow oven (Gas mark 2, Electric 300°F., 150°C.)

# Treacle Tart

*Another old English special which is often forgotten, but always popular. Use treacle or syrup.*

Shortcrust or flaky pastry
2 tablespoons treacle
2 tablespoons breadcrumbs
¼ teaspoon ground ginger

Line a sandwich tin with the pastry, spread over the treacle, mix the breadcrumbs with the ginger and cover the treacle with them. Bake in a hot oven (Gas mark 7, Electric 425°F., 220°C.) for 20 minutes.

# Uncle Tom's Pudding

*I hesitate to guess why this pudding is so named — anyway, if you don't like the name you can always think of another. It is a splendid pudding for the depths of winter — very comforting and warming.*

½ lb. (250 g.) treacle
½ lb. (250 g.) flour
4 oz. (120 g.) suet
2 oz. (60 g.) brown sugar
1 teaspoon ground ginger
1 teaspoon baking soda
1 teaspoon ground cinnamon
1 teaspoon allspice
2 eggs
1 teacup buttermilk

Beat the eggs and mix them with the buttermilk (if you can't get buttermilk, use ordinary milk). Add all the other ingredients, mix very thoroughly and pour into a buttered mould or basin. Cover with greased paper and a pudding cloth, and boil for 2 hours.

# Hunter's Pudding

*This recipe is often to be found in old cookery books and one marvels at its extravagance — one version I found gave 8 eggs in the list of ingredients — and then went on to say that if times were hard, you could omit most of the eggs and substitute a pound of potatoes instead. However, in a more modified form it is a lovely steamed pudding — certainly not for a hot summer's day though.*

10 oz. (300 g.) flour
4 tablespoons breadcrumbs
¼ lb. (120 g.) shredded suet
6 oz. (180 g.) raisins or 4 oz.
    (120 g.) currants
2 oz. (60 g.) brown sugar
1 teaspoon baking powder
Pinch salt
Sour milk (or water) to moisten.

Wash the fruit and pick out any bits. Mix all the dry ingredients thoroughly together and make a rather moist mixture with the sour milk or water. Put into a well-greased pudding basin, cover with greased paper, tie securely with a pudding cloth, and boil for about 3 hours.

# Chocolate Mousse

*A very simple mousse which can be easily expanded or contracted to accomodate any number — as long as eggs are cheap, that is.*

Add a tablespoon of water to the chocolate and melt it over low heat. Stir constantly until the chocolate is completely smooth. Beat the egg yolks and stir the melted chocolate into them. Whip the whites of the eggs very stiffly and fold them over and over into the chocolate mixture so that they are completely blended — this is very important, for the chocolate may otherwise sink to the bottom of the dish. Pour this mixture into a soufflé dish, or other attractive bowl, and leave it to set in a cool place. A few almonds arranged on top after it has set are very attractive.

1 egg per person
1 oz. (30 g.) plain chocolate per
    person

# Bread and Butter Pudding

*This is a favourite with so many people that it would be wrong to leave it out. It is economical, easy, nutritious and so tasty. You can use thinly sliced wholewheat bread if you like, and you can cut the bread into triangular shapes and interleave them in such a way that you have nicely arranged points sticking up all over the top of the pudding — this looks more elegant, but takes a bit longer to do.*

Cut the bread and butter into neat strips and lay them in a buttered pie dish, buttered side up. Sprinkle each layer with fruit and sugar, omitting the fruit on the top layer. Heat the milk and pour it onto the well-beaten egg, strain this mixture over the pie and grate some nutmeg over the top. Stand the dish aside for ½ hour while the bread swells. Bake in a moderate oven (Gas mark 5, Electric 375°F., 190°C.) for about ½ hour, or until set and golden-brown.

3 slices of thin bread and butter
2 oz. (60 g.) currants or
    sultanas
½ oz. (15 g.) sugar
½ pint (300 ml.) milk
1 egg
Nutmeg

# Chocolate Carrot Tart

1 cup steamed carrot, sieved
1 tablespoon sugar
For the pastry:
½ lb. (250 g.) wholewheat flour
3 oz. (90 g.) cooking fat
Water
½ teaspoon vanilla essence
2 tablespoons cocoa

*Curious though this may sound, it is really very good — another wartime special using very little sugar, and containing lots of goodness in the carrots and the wholewheat pastry. People are unlikely to detect the carrot, in fact.*

To make the pastry:
Rub the fat into the flour and add enough water to make a very stiff dough.
Roll out the pastry lightly and line a greased sand-wich tin. Mix the carrots, sugar, cocoa and vanilla thoroughly together and spread this mixture over the pastry — decorate with criss-cross strips of thin pastry and cook in a hot oven (Gas mark 7, Electric 425°F., 220°C.) for about ½ hour, or until the pastry is cooked.

# Krümeltorte

*A German apple cake which is a good one to make when apples are plentiful — cooking apples or eaters may be used. The cake can be served hot or cold, as a dessert or at tea-time. A tin with a loose bottom and hinged sides is the best thing to cook it in, if you have one.*

Wash, peel, core and chop the apples. Partially cook them by simmering without water, but with 2 oz. (60 g.) sugar and 1 teaspoon vanilla essence. Mix the flour with the remaining sugar and another teaspoon vanilla essence, rub in the lard and mix to a stiff dough with the slightly beaten egg. If the dough seems too stiff, add a little cold water. Roll out half the pastry about 1/8 in. thick and cut it to fit the bottom of the tin. Pile the partly-cooked apples on top, but leave a ¼ in. space around the edge. Crumble some of the remaining pastry and let it fall between the apples and the sides of the

2½ lb. (1.25 kg.) apples
4 oz. (120 g.) caster sugar
Vanilla essence
10 oz. (300 g.) self-raising flour
3 oz. (90 g.) lard
1 egg

tin. Smooth the top of the apples and crumble the remaining pastry all over the top. Bake in a moderately hot oven (Gas mark 7, Electric 425°F., 220°C.) for about 25 minutes, until well-browned. Remove the hinged ring, but do not attempt to remove the torte from its base — it would probably break. Sprinkle with caster sugar.

# Lemon Meringue Rice Pudding

*An interesting variation on lemon meringue pie — it takes a while to cook, but is much more acceptable than ordinary rice pudding — instead of the meringue topping you can make a thick caramel with sugar and water which you spread on top of the rice and leave to harden. The dish then becomes Caramel Rice, and should be served very cold.*

Put the washed rice into a double saucepan with the milk and thin lemon rind. Cook gently for about 2 hours until the rice is tender and creamy. Remove the lemon rind and stir in the juice. Allow the mixture to cool slightly and then beat in the egg yolk — add a little sugar to sweeten. Spread a layer of jam on the bottom of a pie dish (if you are making the caramel version it is a good idea to omit the jam, and instead stir in a good tablespoon of chopped candied peel). Pour in the rice mixture. Whisk the egg white stiffly with a dessertspoon of sugar and pile this on top of the rice — sprinkle with a little caster sugar. Bake in a moderate oven (Gas mark 3, Electric 325°F., 170°C.) for 20–30 minutes, until the meringue is lightly browned and crisp. Serve hot. A much quicker version of this dish can be made using left-over boiled rice and starting from where you stir in the lemon juice.

1½ oz. (45 g.) rice
1 pint (600 ml.) milk
Juice and rind of 1 lemon
1 egg
Sugar
Jam

# Mrs Bacon's Plum Pudding

*I came across this Christmas pudding recipe hand-written into the back of an old cookery book kindly lent to me by a friend in our village. It is said to be well over one hundred years old, and uses no eggs. If you wish to add a little brandy, it would certainly do no harm.*

¼ lb. (120 g.) flour
¼ lb. (120 g.) currants
¼ lb. (120 g.) raisins
2 oz. (60 g.) chopped candied peel
5 oz. (150 g.) breadcrumbs
Juice and rind of 1 lemon
Salt
1 teaspoon baking powder
½ teaspoon grated nutmeg
1 teaspoon mixed spice
4 oz. (120 g.) sugar
4 oz. (120 g.) suet
2 oz. (60 g.) grated carrot
1 pint (600 ml.) milk

Mix everything together and leave the mixture to stand for at least 1 hour so that the breadcrumbs will become thoroughly soaked and will swell. Stir thoroughly again, and put the mixture into greased pudding basins. Cover with greased paper and tie firmly with pudding cloths. This pudding should be boiled for about 7 hours altogether. It is best to boil it for 4 hours when you make the puddings, and for a further 3 hours on Christmas Day, or whenever you are going to eat it.

# Water Ices

These ices are very easy to make and can be made with any fruit juice. Among my favourites are blackcurrant and lemon — but if you use black-currants remember to sieve them well to remove all the bits from the juice. You can add egg whites to improve the texture, and this is particularly successful with lemon ice. A good syrup for water ice can be made by boiling together 1 pint (600 ml.) water and 8 oz. (250 g.) sugar. Allow this to cool and then strain in the fruit juice — in general, allow equal quantities of fruit juice and syrup, but these quantities would have to be varied according to the sweetness and flavour of the fruit: the sweeter the fruit, the less syrup. Turn your refrigerater to its lowest setting, put the cold mixture into the freezing tray and allow it to half-freeze (about 1½ hours, usually). Remove the mixture, beat or whisk it well and fold in the stiffly beaten egg white, if you are using one. Return to the freezing tray and leave to freeze, but stir every hour to improve the texture (about 2 hours).

# Mock Cream

2 oz. (60 g.) margarine
2 oz. (60 g.) caster sugar
2 tablespoons boiling water
1 tablespoon top of the milk
A few drops vanilla essence

*Cream continues to increase in price — there is no substitute for it, but as a child I thought that this mock cream was the real thing!*

Cream together the fat and sugar until it is soft and light. Beat in the water a few drops at a time, and then the milk in the same way. Flavour with a little vanilla, beat again and use as required.

# Mrs Fezzard's Mock Cream

1 large cooking apple
Whites of two eggs
½ cup caster sugar
2 or 3 drops vanilla essence

*Mrs. Fezzard lives in the village where I was born and her mock cream, for which she kindly gave me the recipe, became justly famous.*

Peel the apple and grate it very finely. Mix it with the sugar and vanilla and whisk this mixture very thoroughly. Whisk the egg whites stiffly and fold them into the apple with a fork — do not whisk, but beat well with the fork until you have the same consistency as whipped cream. It is very important that the apple mixture should be well whisked before you fold in the egg whites. This cream will discolour if you try to keep it, so make it just before you want to use it.

# Chocolate Mock Cream

1 ½ tablespoons cocoa

2 oz. (60 g.) butter or
    margarine

Approx. 1 tablespoon warm
    water

Vanilla essence

2 oz. (60 g.) sugar

2 level tablespoons soya flour
    or cornflour

Put the butter or margarine in a basin and beat it until it is soft. Add the sugar and cream it until it is light and fluffy. Add the cocoa, flour and water alternatively, beating all the time. Add vanilla essence to taste.

# Baked Alaska

1 tin raspberries

1 sponge cake

Vanilla ice cream

2 egg whites

2 tablespoons sugar

*An American dish for which you could use a stale sponge cake. A very popular sweet with children.*

Put the sponge cake in a fireproof dish. Pour the raspberries over the cake and leave for ½ an hour. Spread the ice cream over the raspberries leaving 1 inch around the edge. Whisk the egg whites, fold in the sugar and pour this meringue mixture over the ice cream making sure that it is completely covered. Bake in a hot oven for 10 minutes.

# Odds & Ends

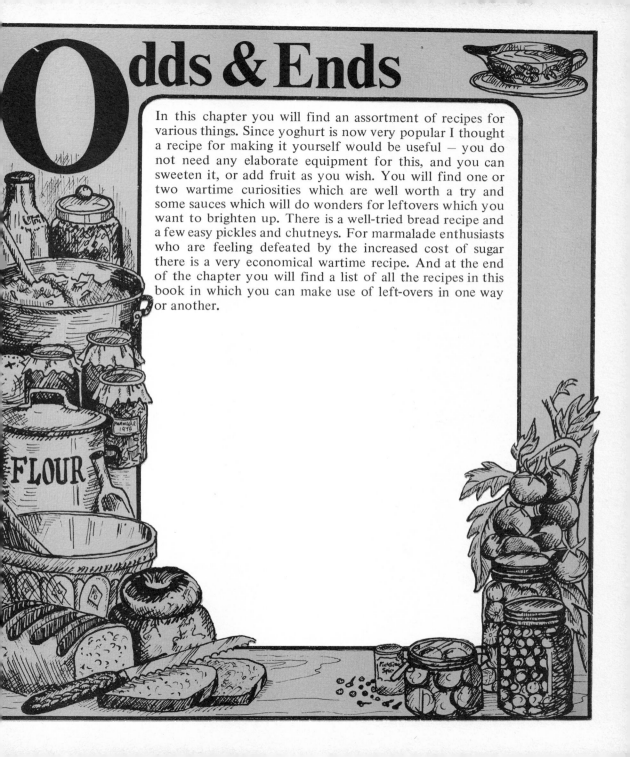

In this chapter you will find an assortment of recipes for various things. Since yoghurt is now very popular I thought a recipe for making it yourself would be useful — you do not need any elaborate equipment for this, and you can sweeten it, or add fruit as you wish. You will find one or two wartime curiosities which are well worth a try and some sauces which will do wonders for leftovers which you want to brighten up. There is a well-tried bread recipe and a few easy pickles and chutneys. For marmalade enthusiasts who are feeling defeated by the increased cost of sugar there is a very economical wartime recipe. And at the end of the chapter you will find a list of all the recipes in this book in which you can make use of left-overs in one way or another.

# To Make Your Own Yoghurt

To make your own plain yoghurt all you need is one tablespoon fresh plain yoghurt (commercially produced) and 1 pint (600 ml.) milk. Pour the milk into a saucepan and bring it to the boil. When it starts to rise to the top of the pan, turn it down and let it simmer for two minutes. Leave it to cool to 106° – 109°F., or 41° – 43°C. (a good way of testing the temperature is to see if you can keep your finger in the milk while you count to ten – if you can, then the temperature should be about right). Remove the skin which will have formed on the milk. Now beat the yoghurt with a fork until it is liquid and add 4 tablespoons of the milk very slowly, beating all the time. Continue adding the milk, still beating, so that it is thoroughly mixed. Cover the bowl with a piece of polythene and secure it with a rubber band. Wrap the bowl in a rug or blanket and put it in a warm draught-free place for 8 hours – an airing cupboard is ideal. When ready the yoghurt should be thick like custard. Cool it in the fridge – you will find that it will keep for a week. If you are using yoghurt in cooking it sometimes tends to curdle – this can be avoided by whisking in 1 tablespoon of cornflour blended with milk.

If you add 1 teaspoon of salt to one pint (600 ml.) of your homemade yoghurt, pour it into a piece of muslin and hang it up overnight to drain, you can use the resulting solid as curd cheese. This cheese is very good with chopped chives or other flavouring mixed into it.

# Sour Milk Cheese

*If by some misfortune you find yourself with a quantity of sour milk, here is a recipe for using it up — a strong tasting Hungarian cheese.*

3 pints (1.8 litres) sour milk
Butter
1 oz. (30 g.) chopped capers
4 anchovies
½ teaspoon chopped onion
1 teaspoon German mustard
1 teaspoon paprika
Salt and pepper

Use the milk when it has become solidified and leave it to drain through muslin for 12 hours. Combine with an equal quantity of butter and when you have a smooth paste add all the other ingredients and season to taste with salt, pepper and paprika.

# Aspic Jelly

*The preparation of a proper aspic jelly is a costly and time-consuming operation, so, unless you use the ready-made packet variety, here is an economic and acceptable alternative.*

½ oz. (15 g.) gelatine
½ pint (300 ml.) boiling water
½ level teaspoon salt
2 level teaspoons caster sugar
2 tablespoons tarragon vinegar
2 tablespoons lemon juice

Dissolve the gelatine in the boiling water and add the other ingredients. If you are going to use it for coating, then allow it to cool and begin to thicken before use.

# Suet Pastry

*Very good for substantial puddings and meat pies — I prefer to put a lid of this pastry on top of a casserole rather than make dumplings.*

8 oz. (250 g.) flour
2 teaspoons baking powder
    (unless you use self-raising
    flour)
1 teaspoon salt
4 oz. (120 g.) suet

Sieve the flour, baking powder and salt together. Chop the suet finely and mix it into the flour. Add enough cold water to make a soft, but not sticky, dough, and use as desired.

# Bread Making

There is one great disadvantage to making your own bread — that is that it is so nice that it is all eaten in no time. Many people prefer to use all wholemeat flour when baking, but this makes the bread too heavy for my taste. In order to get your flour as cheaply as possible, make enquiries to see if there is a mill in your area. I buy mine direct from a fine water-driven mill and the saving is quite considerable — I usually buy 14 lbs. at a time, and I find that bran flour makes the nicest bread. Having taken a long time to produce really good bread — about a year of trying, it seems to me that recipes often omit to tell you rather important things — for example, I find that it is best to leave it to rise for about 2 hours, rather than 1 as most recipes say — don't let it get too hot during this time or you will kill the yeast and have a ghastly failure on your hands. Also, when the dough has risen in the tins, be very careful not to knock the tins as you put them into the oven — this can cause the dough to drop — another reason for failure. Fresh yeast is often hard to get and dried yeast works very well — there is no problem with keeping it, either. This recipe is one that I find works every time:

8 oz. (250 g.) plain flour
8 oz. (250 g.) bran or
    wholemeal flour
1 oz. (30 g.) lard or butter
½ oz. (15 g.) yeast
1 teaspoon sugar
About ½ pint (300 ml.) warm milk

Mix the yeast and the sugar together with about 2 tablespoons of the warm milk. Make sure that it is well mixed, and stand in a warm place for about 10 minutes — at the end of this time it should be all frothy. Sieve the flour and the salt together and stand it in a warm place while you are waiting for the yeast to work. Rub in the fat with your fingers. Add the yeast mixture to the flour and then gradually add the milk until you have a slack dough which is not at all sticky. Knead for about 5 minutes, either on a floured board or in your mixing bowl if it is big enough. I use a large earthenware pancheon for this purpose. Cover the bowl with a damp cloth and leave it until it doubles its bulk — usually about 2 hours in a warm place. Knead the dough again, and put into a greased 1 lb. loaf tin and again leave it in a warm place for about half an hour — by this time it should have risen over the sides of the tin. Preheat the oven to Gas mark 8, Electric 450°F., 230°C. and bake the bread for 15 minutes at this temperature. Then reduce the temperature to Gas mark 5, Electric 375°F., 190°C., and continue to bake for another 15 minutes. When the bread is cooked it should sound hollow if you tap the bottom. Leave it on its side to cool. Be sure to remove it from the tin as soon as it is cooked or it will be soggy.

# Breadcrumbs

It is a complete waste of money to buy these, as everyone finds themselves with stale bread sometimes. Simply rub stale bread through a sieve, and there you are. If you want browned crumbs, put odds and ends of bread into the oven when it is on very low, or is cooling after being switched off. Leave the bread to get thoroughly dry and brown, and then crush it with a rolling pin, or put it into an electric grinder — but don't convert it to dust. These crumbs can be stored in a screw-topped jar. If a recipe calls for a coating of crumbs dotted with butter, it is a good idea to stir fresh breadcrumbs into melted butter first, then spread this mixture over the contents of the dish — this is called Buttered Crumbs.

# Forcemeat Balls

*These balls of stuffing are a very good addition to meat pies, making them much more interesting — if you haven't time to make a forcemeat, you can also use balls of sausage meat. The following is a good basic forcemeat in which the ham or bacon is optional.*

2 oz. (60 g.) suet

1 or 2 oz. (30 − 60 g.) ham or
   bacon

4 oz. (120 g.) fresh breadcrumbs

1 tablespoon chopped parsley

½ teaspoon mixed herbs

Grated rind of ½ a lemon

Salt and pepper

Beaten egg to bind

Chop the suet and ham, if used, and mix well with the breadcrumbs. Add the parsley, herbs and lemon rind, season well and bind with beaten egg. Form into balls for adding to pies, etc., or use for stuffing poultry or rabbits.

# Sage and Onion Stuffing

*This is such a favourite stuffing or forcemeat and the home-made one is so superior to the packet one, that I thought I would include a recipe.*

4 onions

Boiling water

1 oz. (30 g.) butter

4 oz. (120 g.) fresh breadcrumbs

6 sage leaves

1 teaspoon salt

Pepper

Peel the onions, put them in cold water, bring it to the boil and cook for 5 minutes. Strain off this water and cover the onions with fresh boiling water — cook until they are tender. Drain them well and chop finely. Chop the sage leaves finely and mix all the ingredients thoroughly together — it is easiest to soften the butter a little first.

# Savoury Rice

*A useful standby which can be made into a dish on its own with the addition of some chopped ham. Otherwise, it can be served as an accompanying dish with any number of other things. The original Balkan version of this dish calls for pine nuts — not only are these difficult to find, they also tend to be expensive — so use chopped almonds instead.*

8 oz. (250 g.) rice

2 pints (1.2 litres) boiling stock

4 oz. (120 g.) chopped ham

4 oz. (120 g.) dripping

3 finely chopped onions

1 large tomato, chopped and
  peeled

1 oz. (30 g.) sugar

1 teaspoon black pepper

2 teaspoons salt

2 oz. (60 g.) currants

2 oz. (60 g.) chopped almonds

1 teaspoon chopped parsley

1 teaspoon chopped sage

½ teaspoon mixed spice

Melt the fat in a large casserole and cook the chopped onions until soft. Add the nuts and the rice and fry for 5 minutes stirring all the time. Add the salt, pepper currants, tomato, and pour on the boiling stock. Cover the pot with a clean cloth, then the lid, and cook on a very low heat for about 50 minutes, until there is no liquid left. Remove from the heat, stir in the ham, sage, parsley and spice, cover again and leave to stand in a warm place for about 20 minutes before serving.

# To Clarify or Render Down Fat for Frying

*A good way of making your own cooking fat from fatty meat — fat prepared in this way can be used for making plain cakes as well as for frying.*

Remove any discoloured parts or particles of meat from the fat and cut it into small pieces. Put these into a saucepan, cover with cold water, bring to the boil with the lid on for about 30 minutes. This tends to whiten the fat. Remove the lid and boil slowly, removing the scum as it rises to the surface. Continue to boil, stirring from time to time until all the water has evaporated and the liquid looks like clear oil. Let the fat cool and then strain it through a piece of muslin. When cold it will form a firm white cake. Chicken fat rendered in this way is very good for cooking, and can be used instead of butter for frying (see page 103).

# Curry Powder

*If you have the spices in your cupboard, you might like to make up your own curry powder — as long as you don't have to buy the spices specially, then this will be cheaper than buying ready-mixed powder.*

1 teaspoon fenugreek

1 teaspoon poppy seed

2 teaspoons cardomoms

1 tablespoon black peppercorns

2 tablespoons cummin

2 tablespoons turmeric

1 teaspoon mustard seed

2 teaspoons cloves

2 teaspoons chillies

1 tablespoon ground ginger

2 tablespoons coriander

Grind all the seeds together — a coffee grinder is ideal fo this purpose, but do be sure to clean it out properly after use. Mix in the turmeric and ginger thoroughly and store in an airtight jar.

# Wartime Mayonnaise

*I'm afraid there is no economic substitute for the real thing in this case — there is nothing as good as the egg yolk and olive oil mayonnaise. However, I have come across a couple of wartime recipes which are interesting — but I wouldn't call them mayonnaise.*

2 oz. (60 g.) margarine

1 tablespoon wholewheat flour

1 teaspoon dried mustard

3 tablespoons brown sugar

½ pint (300 ml.) milk

1 egg

Raw cooking apple juice, goose-
  berry juice or ¼ pint (150 ml.)
  vinegar

Put the margarine and flour in a double saucepan and allow to melt, stirring well. Remove from heat and add the sugar, mustard and well-beaten egg. Return to the heat and gradually add the milk, stirring all the time. When thick, add the juice or vinegar drop by drop, stirring all the time. Will keep for one week (!).

# Wartime Salad Dressing

1 heaped tablespoon milk (dried)

2 tablespoons water

¼ teaspoon salt

¼ teaspoon sugar

¼ teaspoon pepper

¼ teaspoon dried mustard

1 tablespoon white malt vinegar

Blend the milk, add the other dry ingredients, stir in the vinegar and beat all together until completely smooth.

# Bread Sauce

½ pint (300 ml.) milk

1 onion

6 cloves

1 teacup coarse white bread-
    crumbs

6 peppercorns

1 tablespoon cream or ½ oz.
    (15 g.) butter

*I always think this is a very English sauce — it is very cheap and easy to prepare and goes very well with roast chicken or rabbit.*

Stick the cloves into the peeled onion and simmer it with the peppercorns in the milk for ½ an hour. Remove the onion, add the breadcrumbs, stir in a tablespoon cream or a nut of butter. Reheat.

# Maitre d'Hotel Sauce

4 oz. (120 g.) butter

2 teaspoons finely chopped
    parsley

2 teaspoons lemon juice

Salt and black pepper

*A classic sauce which will add a touch of luxury to the plainest meal.*

With a wooden spoon knead the ingredients together until they are completely smooth.

# Polish Sauce

*A sauce which goes very well with tongue and with boiled meat dishes.*

1¾ oz. (55 g.) butter
2 tablespoons flour
¾ pint (450 ml.) stock
1 oz. (30 g.) sultanas
1 oz. (30 g.) currants
1 oz. (30 g.) blanched almonds
½ wineglass mixed white wine
    and vinegar
3 tablespoons sugar
1½ oz. (45 g.) stale grated
    gingerbread

Make a roux with the butter and the flour, add the stock, stir well and simmer for ½ hour. Strain, add the rest of the ingredients, reheat, and keep warm for about 20 minutes before serving so that the sauce has time to mature. If you haven't got ginger-bread use 1 oz. (30 g.) breadcrumbs with 1 teaspoon ground ginger stirred into them.

# Espagnole Sauce

*A first class sauce to serve with re-heated meat dishes.*

1 large carrot
1 large onion
2 oz. (60 g.) lean bacon
1½ oz. (45 g.) margarine
2 tablespoons flour
½ lb. (250 g.) chopped tomatoes
1 glass white wine
1½ pints (900 ml.) stock
1 bouquet garni made up of
    parsley, thyme and ½ a
    bayleaf

Chop the bacon and the vegetables and brown them in the fat. Sprinkle in the flour, stir well, and cook gently until it is pale brown. Add the stock and cook quickly for about 2 minutes. Then gradually bring the mixture to the boil, stirring well. Add the *bouquet* and simmer, without a lid, for 1 hour, stirring from time to time. Strain into a clean saucepan, squeezing the vegetables to extract all the juice, then simmer for another ½ hour. Although it takes some time to prepare it is an invaluable aid to dressing up cooked left-overs.

# Avgolemono Sauce

*A lovely sauce which the Greeks serve with practically any meat dish — it goes particularly well with rissoles and dolmas. The method of preparing it was shown to me by a very good friend in Athens when we spent a few days of gastronomic delight with her.*

½ pint (300 ml.) chicken stock
2 egg yolks
Juice of 1 lemon

It is best to make this in a double saucepan so that it does not boil and cause the eggs to curdle. Heat the stock. Beat the egg yolks with the lemon juice, pour on the very hot stock and stir until it thickens.

# Basic White Sauce

Many different sauces can be made by the addition of flavouring to a basic white sauce. Make your basic sauce by stirring ½ oz. (15 g.) flour into ½ oz. (15 g.) melted butter, and slowly adding ½ pint (300 ml.) milk, stirring it until it thickens. Season to taste and then add flavourings in the proportions given below.

**Anchovy Sauce**

1 teaspoon anchovy essence per ½ pint (300 ml.) white sauce.

**Caper Sauce**

1 dessertspoon chopped capers and a little of the caper vinegar per ½ pint (300 ml.)

**Cheese Sauce**

1 oz. (30 g.) grated cheese and 1 teaspoon made mustard per ½ pint (300 ml.)

**Egg Sauce**

1 hard-boiled egg, roughly chopped per ½ pint (300 ml.)

**Mustard Sauce**

1 teaspoon mustard mixed with 1 dessertspoon vinegar per ½ pint (300 ml.)

**Onion Sauce**

1 large cooked onion, chopped finely per ½ pint (300 ml.)

**Parsley Sauce**

1 tablespoon finely chopped parsley per ½ pint (300 ml.).

# Thick Tomato Sauce

1 small onion
1 tablespoon olive oil
½ oz. (15 g.) butter
1 lb. (500 g.) ripe tomatoes
1 clove garlic (optional)
Salt and freshly ground black
    pepper
Lump of sugar
Chopped parsley, celery leaves
    or dried basil

Melt the oil and butter together in a heavy pan. Finely chop the onion and the garlic (if you are using it) and fry gently for about 5 minutes. Roughly chop the tomatoes and add them to the onion and season with salt, pepper and a lump of sugar. Add the parsley, celery or basil and simmer until the tomatoes are soft and thick. Sieve, and if the sauce is too runny, return it to the pan to dry out a bit. A mixture of parsley and celery leaves is also good in this sauce.

# A Few Pickles

Home-made pickles and chutneys are always popular and are quickly and easily prepared — they are also useful in using up gluts of fruit or vegetables.

# Pickled Onions

*Quite the simplest way of pickling onions that I have come across — it originally comes from an old edition of Mrs. Beeton's Englishwoman's Cookery Book. As the vinegar is used cold, the onions are beautifully crunchy, and will keep for about six months.*

Pickling onions:
To each 2 pints (1.2 litres) of vinegar allow 2 teaspoons allspice and 2 teaspoons black peppercorns. You can also add 2 pieces root ginger and two dried chillies, but this is not essential.
Peel the onions so that they look quite clean and white making sure that you remove that very thin skin which lies between the layers. Put them into dry jars as soon as they are peeled and pour in

sufficient cold vinegar to cover them making sure
that the spices are added in the correct proportion
to each jar. Cover them securely and they will be
ready to eat in a fortnight.

# Scottish French Mustard

2 teaspoons dry mustard
4 teaspoons salt
4 teaspoons caster sugar
4 teaspoons melted butter
½ teaspoon cayenne pepper
The juice of 1 raw onion, or
    the whole onion finely
    chopped
Vinegar

*This can be prepared in minutes and is guaranteed
to take the top of your head off! It will keep for
about a year but is only for those who like their
pickles strong.*

Mix all the ingredients together thoroughly, making
sure that there are no lumps. Add sufficient vinegar
to make the desired consistency and put into small
jars. Cover securely.

# Green Gooseberry Chutney

2 lbs. (1 kg.) green gooseberries
½ pint (300 ml.) vinegar
1 teaspoon ground ginger
1 teaspoon ground cinnamon
1 teaspoon grated nutmeg
1 teaspoon cloves
1 teaspoon allspice
1 lb. (500 g.) sugar

Top and tail the gooseberries. Boil together the
vinegar, the ginger, cinnamon, nutmeg, cloves,
allspice and sugar for 10 minutes. Add the gooseberries and boil for 20 minutes or until thick. Pour
into dry jars and cover securely.

# Marrow Chutney

4 lb. (2 kg.) vegetable marrow
3 pints (1.8 litres) malt vinegar
1½ oz. (45 g.) mustard
½ lb. (250 g.) lump sugar
6 cloves
6 chillies
½ oz. (15 g.) turmeric
½ lb. (250 g.) onions

Cut the marrow into small even pieces, put them in a basin and sprinkle with salt. Leave overnight and squeeze out the moisture next day. Chop the onions very finely and put them into a pan with the marrow and all the other ingredients. Bring to the boil and cook gently for about ½ hour, stirring from time to time. Put into jars and cover as for jam.

# Spiced Green Tomatoes

3 lb. (1.5 kg.) small green tomatoes
Salt
½ lb. (250 g.) sugar
1 pint (600 ml.) vinegar
1 tablespoon pickling spices

*This makes a change from green tomato chutney, and the smaller the tomatoes are the better.*

Put the spices into the vinegar and bring to the boil. Leave to stand for 1½ hours and then strain the vinegar for use. Wipe the tomatoes and remove the green stalks, then prick them about six times. Put them in a bowl and sprinkle them thickly with salt. Leave them for about 12 hours, then wash off the salt. Bring the spiced vinegar to boil in a large pan, drop the tomatoes in and let them simmer for 20 minutes. Do not stir them or you will break them. Drain them and put them into dry jars. Boil up the liquid and pour it over the tomatoes, making sure that they are covered. Cover securely.

# Preserving Tomatoes

The price of tomatoes fluctuates considerably, the prices being so high at times as to make them almost a luxury item. So when they are cheap, why not bottle some for use in cooking — they will keep for a long time. You can skin them or not as you wish. They should be packed neatly in to the preserving jars and sprinkled with salt and sugar in the proportion of 2 level teaspoons salt and 1 level teaspoon sugar to each 2 lb. (1 kg.) tomatoes. Cover the jars with saucers and sterilize them in a very slow oven (Gas mark ¼, Electric 225°F., 110°C.) for 2 hours. They may shrink considerably, in which case you should fill one jar from another. If you have to do this, put them back into the oven for a further 10 minutes. Remove the jars from the oven one by one and fill each with boiling water. Seal the jars in accordance with the instructions — there are various kinds of preserving jars available. As the jars are cooling, tighten metal screws if these are the type of jars you are using. Next day test the jars to make sure they are properly sealed — remove screw bands or clips and lift the jar by the lid — if the lid comes off the jar is not sealed and you will either have to use up the tomatoes at once, or sterilize them again.

# Tomato Store Sauce

*Another good thing to make when tomatoes are really cheap — you can use very ripe ones for this and it is much nicer than the ready made sauce you can buy.*

4 lb. (2 kg.) ripe tomatoes

½ lb. (250 g.) shallots

½ oz. (15 g.) salt

A pinch cayenne

½ teaspoon paprika

4 oz. (120 g.) sugar

1/3 pint (200 ml.) spiced vinegar (see page 180, Spiced Green Tomatoes)

Wash the tomatoes and cut them up. Peel and slice the shallots. Put tomatoes and shallots into a pan and stir them over a very low heat for a few minutes. Then bring to the boil and allow to simmer gently until cooked and thick. Rub through a sieve and return to a pan with all the other ingredients. Boil and stir constantly until you have a nice creamy consistency. Sterilize some bottles and corks in boiling water for ½ hour and pour the sauce into the hot bottles.

Cork the bottles, and when the sauce is cold, seal by dipping the necks into melted paraffin wax.

# Wartime Marmalade

*A lot of people like to make their own marmalade, but one of the problems now is to get the right kind of oranges at the right price, and to get, and afford, the quantity of sugar normally required. This is how wartime cooks overcame these difficulties.*

Soak the oranges in the cold water for 24 hours. Put the rind and the water into a saucepan, bring to the boil and simmer for 1 hour, or until the rind is soft. Remove the rind and shred it. Keep the water. Do not peel or core the apples, just wash them and cut them into quarters. Make up the water to 3 pints (1.8 litres) and cook the apples in it until they are soft. Pour the entire contents of the pan into a piece of muslin in a colander and leave to drip until well drained — do not be tempted to squeeze the muslin during this process or the juice will go cloudy. Add ¾ lb. (360 g.) sugar to each pint of this juice. Pour into a pan and bring to the boil. Boil briskly for 20 minutes and a couple of minutes before the boiling is finished remove the scum from the top. Stir in the shredded orange rind and allow to cool slightly before you pour the marmalade into hot jars and cover as for jam.

**Rind of 3 oranges**
**3 pints (1.8 litres) water**
**3 lbs. (1.5 kg.) cooking apples**
**¾ lb. (360 g.) sugar to every**
    **pint (600 ml.) juice**

# Leftovers

If you habitually find yourself with a lot of food left after every meal, then you should ask yourself two questions: are you constantly buying and cooking more food than you need; or, even worse, are you cooking it badly? If the answer to the first question is 'yes', then try to plan more efficiently

— I find it best to plan menus a week in advance if possible. If the answer to the second question is 'yes', then I hope this book will help to rectify the situation!

However, even in the best-run households there are some left-overs and, where possible, these should be incorporated into other dishes so that they are not wasted. Of course, you may intentionally cook for more than one meal at a time — for example, if one day you are cooking boiled potatoes and the next day you plan to cook a dish that will need mashed potatoes (such as Fish Timbale — page 64), then cook enough potatoes on the first day for both meals. When dealing with legitimate left-overs you should cool them as rapidly as possible after the meal and store them, lightly wrapped in a fridge or cold larder. But don't try to keep them too long — it's really safest to try to use them up the next day, although you can keep most meat for a couple of days with safety. When reheating meat always bring it to the boil to destroy any harmful micro-organisms — warming is not sufficient as this encourages the growth of micro-organisms. And it is a good idea to serve a fresh vegetable or salad with a made-up dish to compensate for the loss of nutritional value in the first cooking.

In general, vegetable trimmings can be used for stock as can bones and meat trimmings. Fat can be rendered down (see page 173). The following list will direct you to recipes in the book in which left-overs can be used, and also includes a few other suggestions.

# Fish

Left-over fish can be used in a variety of ways — to make fish cakes or kedgeree, or it can be mixed with diced celery, lemon juice and oil, diced cucumber and mayonnaise to make a fish salad. For kedgeree you should melt some butter in a saucepan, add the flaked fish, cooked rice (2 cupfuls for 1½ cupfuls of fish, finely chopped hard-boiled eggs, and paprika and nutmeg to taste — serve piping hot.

It can also be used in:

Savoury Fish (p. 14)

Eggs Benedictine (p. 45)

Whiting Soufflé (p. 62)

# Meat

There are many ways in which you can use left-over meat — it can be curried; reheated in a casserole with a good sauce; minced finely and mixed with a little butter to make fillings for sandwiches; chopped and added to soups or to stuffings; and cold roast meat, if in sufficient quantity, can be sliced and served with a fresh green or vegetable salad. Cold meat can also be used in the following recipes:

Potted Meat (p. 19)

Meat Sanders (p. 18)

Italian Vegetable soup (p. 29)

Jellied Moulds (p. 72)

Ravioli (p. 74)

Lamb Patties (p. 86)

The Cabbage of My House (p. 124)

Cauliflower a l'Italienne (p. 129)

Stuffed Peppers (p. 139)

Stuffed Potatoes (p. 140)

Left-over *pork* can be used in:

Potted Meat (bacon) (p. 19)

Scalloped Pork (p. 78)

Left-over *lamb* can be used in:
Suliman's Pilaff (p. 82)
Lamb Patties (p. 86)
German Cutlets (p. 84)

Cold *chicken* is very good served with a nice salad,
and of course, the carcase and giblets are particularly
good for stocks and gravies. The following recipes
use cold chicken:
Potted Chicken (p. 19)
Chicken Broth (p. 29)
Chicken Pilaff (p. 105)
Devilled Chicken (p. 105)
Chicken with Cream (p. 106)

Left-over *turkey* can be used in:
Devilled Turkey Legs (p. 107)
Savoury Turkey Border (p. 107)
Turkey Cigars (p. 108)

Left-over cold *tongue* can be used in the following
ways:
Cold Tongue (p. 100)
Cauliflower a l'Italienne (p. 129)

Cold *liver* can be minced and mixed with melted
butter and seasoning to make a very good sandwich
filling.

# Vegetables

Boiled root vegetables may be diced and mixed with
mayonnaise to make vegetable salad, or they can be
mashed and sieved and used as the basis for cream
soups. Cold boiled potatoes are excellent sliced,
mixed with a little finely chopped garlic, and sautéed.

And don't forget Bubble and Squeak (strictly, fried slices of boiled beef and a cake of mixed left-over potatoes and greens, also fried — but the name is now more frequently given just to the fried vegetable mixture).

When you are preparing cauliflower, don't throw away the outer leaves — cut out the thick central stems, trim them evenly and simmer them for about 30 minutes in boiling salted water, then serve them with melted butter and black pepper as an hors d'oeuvre. Put the outer skins of onions into stock or soup to give colour and flavour, and use the green tops of onions as a garnish (chopped finely). Don't throw away the leaves from a bunch of celery, they are very good for flavouring — likewise the coarse green tops of leeks.

Vegetable left-overs can also be used in the following recipes:

Meat Sanders (mashed potato) (p. 18)
Leek and Potato Soup (leek tops) (p. 28)
Italian Vegetable Soup (p. 29)
Pea Pod Soup (p. 26)
Split Pea Soup (celery) (p. 31)
Macaroni and Egg Casserole (beans) (p. 37)
Macaroni and Cheese Timbale (mashed potato) (p. 42)
Pain de choufleur (p. 128)
Potato and Cheese Mould (p. 140)

# Miscellaneous

Cold boiled *rice* can be added to vegetable or fish soups, or it can be added to stuffings (Peppers — p. 139), or used for sweets (p. 163).

*Sour milk* is very useful for making scones, as well as cheese (p. 169).

*White of egg* can be whisked and added to cream to make it go further, while *yolks* can be added to omelettes, or stirred into soups (which should not be allowed to boil afterwards).

Use *stale bread* to make breadcrumbs (p. 171), or in Simple Soufflé (p. 38), or in Almundigoes (p. 72).

Add left-over *sauces* to appropriate soups or stews, and white sauce can be flavoured in a variety of different ways (p. 177).

*Orange peel* can be used to make Wartime Marmalade (p. 182), or it can be candied as follows:
Wash, dry, and cut the peel into narrow strips. Put them in a pan covered with cold water and bring slowly to the boil. Drain them, add fresh water, bring to the boil again. Drain again, add fresh water and repeat the boiling and draining process. Put the rind into a thick pan, add an equal quantity of sugar and just enough boiling water to cover. Simmer until the rind is clear and tender, cool it, drain it and roll it in caster sugar. Spread the strips on waxed paper to dry and the next day roll in caster sugar again. Lemon and grapefruit peel can be candied in the same way, but they should be soaked in cold water overnight to extract some of the bitterness — they should then be drained well before you start the boiling processes.

I am sure there are many other ways in which you can use up left-overs imaginatively — it is worth giving the matter some thought, as it is an excellent way of economising. But remember that if you have to go out and buy a lot of expensive ingredients to make some scraps palatable, it is not worth it.

# Index